"Jamie is the only Christian writer I know who doesn't filter her thoughts and words through an 'appropriateness meter,' so her memoir is original, hilarious, and believable. Jamie shows that a woman can be full of contradictions, full of fire, and full of faith—all at same time. If you find yourself losing your religion, read this brilliant book before you bail. It's possible to be thinking, honest, inclusive, relevant, compelling, compassionate *and* Christian—Jamie's proof."

—Glennon Doyle, author of the #1 *New York Times* bestseller *Love Warrior* and founder of Together Rising

"This book is one of the smartest, funniest, and truest books on faith I've ever read. *The Very Worst Missionary* will draw you in and keep you thinking. It will remind you that, even when you think you're at your worst, you're not alone."

—Rachel Held Evans, *New York Times* bestselling author of *A Year of Biblical Womanhood* and *Searching for Sunday*

"This book might make you clutch your pearls, or laugh out loud, or angry. It might break your heart. Maybe all of the above. But at least you won't remain unmoved by Jamie's profound, wise, and funny-as-hell story. Jamie's love for the church is ferocious and refining, and we desperately need to read and heed this book."

—Sarah Bessey, author of *Jesus Feminist* and *Out of Sorts*

"Think of *The Very Worst Missionary* as the literary lovechild of Mother Teresa and Sarah Silverman—a crass-and-light-filled narrative that will have you laughing one minute and looking in the mirror the next. We need this book in the very worst way."

—Matthew Paul Turner, author of *Churched* and *When God Made You*

"If you've lived and worked abroad, I predict you will nod your head in recognition as Jamie takes on the sacred cows of Christian missions with honesty, humor, and not a religious platitude in sight."

—Tara Livesay, director of Heartline Ministries, Haiti

"Jamie had me howling with laughter and cringing with recognition at her earnest and yet misguided endeavor to save the world. Equal parts memoir and scathing but self-deprecating critique, *The Very Worst Missionary* shows how even our best intentions can go awry and how we can find our way again."

—Kristen Howerton, author of *Rage Against the Minivan*

"Rip-roaringly funny, brutally honest, and so very endearing . . . an absolute joy to read from first page to last."

—Nish Weiseth, author of *Speak: How Your Story Can Change the World*

"We've traveled with Jamie into red-light districts in Asia, where we've seen how she's been able to use her voice to advocate for the most vulnerable. In *The Very Worst Missionary*, she hosts a conversation that globally minded people of faith absolutely *need*."

—Matt and Laura Parker, founders of The Exodus Road

"Gritty, funny, and thoughtful . . . all the things faith should be but rarely is. I love Jamie's story, her voice, and the way she looks at the world. After you read this, I'm confident you will, too."

—Jeff Goins, author of *The Art of Work*

"Jamie writes with eloquence, humility, and snark (no doubt a spiritual gift). Everyone should read this brave book."

—Emily Worrall, co-creator of Barbie Savior

"I've never seen a fellow Christian write with such courage, authenticity, and balance. You will come away feeling that your hurts and frustrations have been validated, and motivated to love bigger."

—Benjamin L. Corey, author of *Unafraid*

"Jamie brings the wit of Joan Rivers, the pen of Mary Carr, and the spirit of a prophet. This is one of those rare religious books that makes you feel okay with who you are while inspiring you to want to be better."

—Caleb Wilde, author of *Confessions of a Funeral Director*

"Jamie gives us permission to admit just how screwed up we really are and accept how much God loves us anyway. One of the best, most refreshing books I've read in a very long time."

—Zack Hunt, writer, blogger, and preacher

THE VERY WORST MISSIONARY

A Memoir or Whatever

JAMIE WRIGHT

CONVERGENT BOOKS
NEW YORK

Published in the United States by Convergent Books, an imprint
of the Crown Publishing Group, a division of Penguin Random
House LLC, New York.
crownpublishing.com

CONVERGENT BOOKS is a registered trademark and its
C colophon is a trademark of Penguin Random House LLC.

Library of Congress Cataloging-in-Publication Data is available
upon request.

ISBN 978-0-451-49653-9
Ebook ISBN 978-0-451-49654-6

Printed in the United States of America

Cover design by Emily Mahon
Cover photography: Claudia Below/plainpicture

10 9 8 7 6 5 4 3 2 1

First Edition

For Steve.

Thank you for the office.

And, also, for everything else.

And for Stephen, Dylan, and Jamison.

Sorry about dragging you off to live in a foreign country.

It honestly seemed like a good idea at the time.

CONTENTS

Jamie teases me good-naturedly about my annoying optimism. It is the actual worst. I'll readily admit to being the dumb girl who thinks the arsonist holding the gasoline can was probably just on his way to help a stranded driver. Jamie grew up Jew-ish and then not; I grew up with flannel boards about Noah and the Ark in Southern Baptist Sunday school. We took two different paths to Jesus but both set out to save the world with our well-intentioned zest for evangelism. We both tried really, really hard to follow the church rules and protect our good standing. We each did the things and said the words and took the trips and prayed the prayers.

And that cynic and this optimist found ourselves in the same disillusioned spiritual space.

I think that is why: 1) Jamie and I are super close—like, real-life-talk-nearly-every-day friends, and 2) I devoured this book in one sitting, oscillating between violent laughter and a settle-in-your-bones relief at being so understood. The reason you love Jamie (or are about to) is because she says exactly what the rest of us are thinking, but we're too afraid to upset the apple cart. The spiritual garbage we pander to or justify or even perpetuate can't escape Jamie's direct line of questioning. She lays it bare, exposing our subculture where it is harmful instead of helpful, fake instead of genuine, full of crap instead of full of Jesus.

I love my girl not just because of her saucy mouth and outrageous snark but because this broken-down world and our busted-up human hearts deserve better than a list of rules and a church that emphasizes *fitting in* over *true belonging*. When Jamie talks about Jesus, I can't think of a better way to put it than this: I recognize Him. That is the Jesus I know, the one that the Bible describes, the one I love enough to hand over my entire life. When everything about the church and church people crumbles around me, when there doesn't feel like a safe spot on planet Earth, Jesus still feels safe to me. Jamie and I follow the same Jesus, and in that way, this book is profoundly nurturing. You might cry tears of relief as I did.

A note of high praise to Jamie: even in the midst of dismantling, she honors the church where she found Jesus and all the folks thriving in that spiritual environment. She avoids taking easy shots at motives, character, or sincerity. I think this matters. Conventional Christian spaces have their place in her story, and she describes them with humor and generosity. But the straight-up gift of God on Jamie's life is that she has eyes to see what hundreds of thousands of us need outside those tidy walls—*a faith for the rest of us.* She is a voice for the outlier, and we're famished for what she has to say.

I trust Jamie for many reasons, but at the core of it, I know without any doubt that she is always, always telling the truth. Increasingly, this matters. I can no longer bear hearing one thing coming out of a leader's mouth while the evidence makes plain another reality. I'm hypersensitive to agendas, party lines, Christianese, and power. I have no room for talking points, blacklisting, spiritual manipulation, or authoritarianism. Spare me your shame-based gospel, judgment, thinly veiled hatred, and arrogance. That used to be my banquet table, and it left me starved. I need truth and vulnerability, and I need my leaders to call something broken when it is instead of dousing it with spiritual sugar to help it go down. I need fearlessness, which is increasingly rare. When possible, I need spicy messaging, and I'm here to deliver some good news to you, reader: you shall receive that in spades herein.

This is a book for the rest of us. There are so many of us, dear ones. Be encouraged. This growing band of ragamuffins and scalawags and ne'er-do-wells and good-hearted rebels are finding a new space, finding a new voice, finding Jesus despite all odds, thriving spiritually in places declared unfit with people labeled unworthy, and it is a beautiful mess. You are so welcome here. You are incredibly loved by Jesus, and in Jamie, you will find a trustworthy guide to lead you through the pits of loss, failure, sadness, all the way to redemption.

All the way home.

Jen Hatmaker
Author of *For the Love* and the *New York Times* bestseller *Of Mess and Moxie*

This Book Might Kinda Suck

Sorry.

I just need to get this apology out of the way before you dive into this book with any sort of expectations and end up feeling disappointed because you were somehow misled to believe this would be a good book. Or a meaningful book. Or a helpful book. If we're lucky, it will have a couple of decent readable parts, and that would be a nice surprise for both of us. But if you read this thing and it ends up taking a literary dump on your soul, feel free to run straight to the Internet and leave a sad little one-star review that says, "This book sucks."

Fair warning: If you do that, the reasonable people who leave good reviews (because they're nice and cool and extremely good-looking) will be like, "Hey, chump, it says it sucks on, like, *the very first page! What kind of monster gives a one-star review to a book that delivers* exactly *what it promised?!*" And then you'll look like an asshole. So if you hate this book, the only way for you to come out on top would be for you to leave a five-star review *agreeing* that I was absolutely right about my book sucking and that you're just grateful I told you right at the beginning. I mean, that's what an honest, fair, generally decent human being would do. But hey, *you do you.*

Anyway.

I realize this is probably weird, since most authors don't start their books off with an apology, so bear with me. This is just a thing I do—I'm a compulsive preapologizer. Like, if I invite you to my house for dinner, I will spend the day cleaning and scrubbing and shoving crap into drawers until the whole house shines like a new penny and then, when you arrive, I will apologize as you walk through the door, "Hi, come on in! *Sorry about the mess.*"

I cannot help it. It's, like, my solemn duty to warn you about my potential inadequacy in advance, because only after I've sufficiently lowered your expectations and opened the wine can we all sit back, relax, and have a nice time. The riskier the situation, the more apologetic I feel, and inviting you into a book about my life and faith and failure feels a lot riskier than letting you taste my lasagna or use my toilet.

I think anyone who has experienced a major personal or theological shift can understand exactly why book writing freaks me the fuck out. It's because our beliefs tend to change over time, so much that in many ways I'm not even the same person I was when I first fell in love with Jesus. I mean, if I met 1998 Christian me, with her gold-cross necklace and her mom bob and her cheap, cheesy platitudes today? I'd probably give her the finger.

That's the inherent problem with writing a book centered on life and faith. It's that, in the end, my own perception of God is subjective and insufficient and ever changing. I'm still in the middle of this process and I will undoubtedly continue to change, but this book won't be changing with me. In ten years this is all just gonna be a big fat public record of how dumb I was when I wrote it, so I might as well just get the apologies out of the way right now.

The other problem is that two people never remember a single event the exact same way; this is a scientific fact I've observed personally many times in over twenty years of marriage. But the reality of writing a memoir is this: All of the people in this book really exist and all of this stuff really happened. These pages are filled with true stories and fake names, shared memories and personal perceptions, deeply felt convictions and loosely held ideas, and there's a strong likelihood that I will get some of it wrong, historically or theologically or both.

But I like people who tell me the truth and I try to be someone who tells the truth, even (maybe especially) when it's unflattering, because I believe the honest truth is like an invitation into another person's soul. Lies hide us, secrets isolate us, partial truths confine us, but through the most blatant and bare honesty we are fully known, genuinely connected, and utterly freed. I'm here to tell the whole truth, no matter how scary that seems.

I once went to a circus and watched a group of acrobats fly and flip and snatch one another out of the air with nothing but their half-naked bodies and chalky bare hands. The performance was beautiful and terrifying, and their demonstration of skill, strength, and grace had everyone in the audience gasping and squirming. At the end of the routine, the flyers dropped, one by one, into a safety net below, and nobody was shocked or disappointed that it was there to catch them. The net didn't detract from the artistry of their act, it didn't take away from their athletic prowess, and neither did it guarantee their well-being—but it did free them to fly higher, to risk bigger, to try something braver.

I think that's a pretty good approach to life. Sometimes a safety net is simply an acknowledgment of our capacity to make mistakes. Sometimes we slip. Sometimes we get it wrong. Sometimes we misjudge. Sometimes we write a book that sucks ass. The safety net is there to make us brave enough to step out in the first place. It's there to remind us that even if we completely bomb, it'll be okay, and we'll *probably* even live through it.

It's arrogance that puffs us up and says, "I've got this. I know what I'm doing." But humility casts a net. Humility sees us in all of our imperfection, stretches a wide net beneath us, and gently urges us to move out over whatever terrible abyss we're facing.

For me, writing this book is my own half-naked high-wire act, and it feels kind of crazy, but I'm doing it anyway.

So this is me preapologizing for all the parts I get wrong.

This is me weaving a little safety net to make me brave.

This is me inching out over the abyss, despite fear, to share the story of living out faith, despite failure.

Come on in. Sorry about the mess.

PART 1
The Odd Early Years

1
The Very Worst Missionary

The year I turned thirty-two, I took a deep breath and marched boldly into full-time ministry as a missionary to Costa Rica. I wasn't alone in this soul-saving, world-changing, God-pleasing endeavor—my husband, Steve, and our three sons (thirteen, nine, and seven at the time) were also in on this adventure. People often assume that our kids must be oh so grateful to have been given the gift of worldly perspective during their early years, so allow me to dispel that fantasy. Today, as young adults, our children all agree we pretty much ruined their lives by dragging them off to a faraway land, saddling them with a second language, and forcing upon them a great variety of new people, places, and cultures. But, in their defense, our life overseas was kind of a shit show.

Steve and I intentionally gave up every ounce of stability we'd enjoyed in the United States, said good-bye to our community, and took a massive financial hit to chase a dream of being a small part of something big. We were acting on what we'd been taught: that the world needs missionaries to find the lost, feed the hungry, heal the sick, and free the enslaved. And, for a minute, it honestly seemed that simple.

Everyone kept saying how *awesome* everything about missions was and how *amazing* we were for our willingness to take our family and go, and I happily, willfully believed them. Imagine my dismay when I finally came face to face with this thing called Christian missions and what I found was actually countless ways in which things were not awesome or amazing.

Costa Rica was a tiny Catholic country practically overrun with North American Evangelicals, many of whom were arrogant, lazy, inconsiderate, manipulative, and self-absorbed. The work of missionaries was often subpar or nonexistent, wasteful, and, at times, even *harmful* to the local culture and economy. But the pervading understanding was that every missionary, including me, was called by God, and that through our mere presence and our important "work" we were changing the world. When Steve and I flew away to play house in another country, we'd built a whole new life on this premise, which almost immediately I began to suspect was false, or at the very least deeply flawed.

I wanted to talk about the questions and doubts I was having, but I didn't know how people would respond if I started to pick away at the accepted narrative that all missions are good missions and all missionaries are good missionaries. There seemed to be a great deal of evidence to the contrary, but could I dare to tell a different story?

In the spirit of self-preservation, I could sit here and say, "The truth is, I saw a lot of unfit missionaries doing unnecessary stuff, which made me uncomfortable." But the *whole truth* is that I wrestled with the broad practice of Christian missions, in part because I was a hot mess of a missionary, a perfect example of at least a dozen things that are wrong with the system. And I knew that if I were to expose the ugly truths I'd seen, I would have to acknowledge that I'd seen a lot of them in me.

———

I curled up in a ball and sucked my thumb, while Steve took to life in Costa Rica like a hot chick to Coachella.

His daily grind as the director of buildings and operations for our organization's Latin American headquarters came with a never-ending list of things to do. Between new projects and old maintenance on the ministry campus, a steady flow of work allowed him to dive right into friendly relationships with landscapers, construction workers, contractors, and every single human being who worked at a hardware or building-supply store within a twenty-mile radius. It wasn't long before everywhere we went someone came up to shake hands and say hello to the big, friendly gringo with the bad accent who worked up on the mountain.

Unabashed, industrious, openhanded, and approachable; in so many ways, Steve was a very good missionary.

And I was just like him, but, like, *the complete opposite.*

When I had to psych myself up just to put on pants and go out for laundry detergent, Steve was braving the packed corridors of the dingy government hospital in Alajuela, because he had learned he could donate blood to offset the cost of a transfusion for his building foreman's wife. While I was thinking of ways to avoid talking to taxi drivers more than absolutely necessary, Steve was getting to know local shop owners and their employees by name. While I stuck strictly to the routes, rituals, and cultural rules I knew and trusted, he made a point of exploring and experiencing everything he possibly could. I was envious of how easily Steve transitioned into life in Costa Rica, and he was truly baffled that it wasn't as easy for me.

Since I was practically a hermit without much on my plate and Steve was always busy with one thousand things, I quietly took over the unofficial role of communications director for our clan. I'd never written anything in my life, but from my favorite spot on the sofa, I could keep our family, friends, and supporters filled in on our wild and wacky day-to-day lives. It was my responsibility to make sure updates included dramatic shots of three pasty white boys in a sea of brown people, and artsy pics of fresh produce, weird cuts of meat, and towers of pirated DVDs for sale under brightly colored tarps at the Saturday-morning markets. Snapshots of brilliant sunsets, torrential rainfalls, stray dogs with hilarious underbites, and oxcarts blocking traffic also served well to help me tell our story.

Along with a few of those "look at our crazy life" pics, our first update went out with an image of my smiling husband, submerged waist deep in a swimming pool with his arm around the Costa Rican guy he'd just helped baptize. It was taken on our very first Sunday in the country at a baptism that just happened to be occurring in the private swimming pool where we stayed. Our family stumbled across this celebration, completely by accident, on a morning walk across the property, and a Canadian missionary generously invited Steve to join right in with the dunking. It seemed like the missionaryish thing to do, so he did.

In the update, I shared how God was already using us in *awesome* and *amazing* ways. The story was carefully worded so as not to mislead anyone into thinking we'd done anything more than just arrive at a baptism in progress, but I did choose that picture and tell that story because it felt appropriately interesting for would-be investors, and it was an optimistic way to show supporters that the Wright family was a wise choice for their missionary money. We never saw the baptized guy again, but he sure gave us something to write home about, which is lucky, because writing home is key to a missionary's livelihood.

Now we cringe so hard at that picture, having since developed ethical objections to the use of people as fodder for the Christian-Missions Machine. After seeing firsthand the troubling results of foreigners engaged in exactly that kind of drive-by ministry, today Steve would not agree to join in, but the eagerness he showed that day, that willingness to jump right in, is exactly the kind of thing that made him a really good missionary.

I did not cannonball into a stranger's baptism. Instead, as the family's communications director, I summarized our new life as missionaries and promised readers great adventures to come. I must have been feeling very precious the day I tapped out my first blog post, because I wrapped it up with a single sentence that would come back to mock me.

"I am pleased to report that being a missionary is pretty darn cool."

Sweet Jesus. Was I high when I wrote that? I don't know. All I know is that eighteen months later, I couldn't have disagreed more.

The rose-colored glasses I wore flouncing into the mission field quickly shattered and (metaphorically speaking) stabbed me in the eyeballs. I was dying to tell the truth about messed-up missions and messy me. . . . The question was, how could I break the bad news to all those people who still believed that everything missions was awesome and amazing? Should I just admit that I'd been totally wrong? Being a missionary *wasn't* pretty darn cool; *it was super goddamn hard*. But was I allowed to say that? Could I share what I had learned during my first year and a half in Costa Rica: that, nope, it's not enough to just show up ignorant and ill prepared and expect God to work miracles? Could I say something about the alarming number of weirdos, jackasses, and dipshits out there who were also called missionaries? I just wasn't sure what would happen if I publicly suggested that maybe God and the world deserved so much better.

I gave all of this two whole minutes of serious consideration, and then I thought, *Fuck it. Who am I here to impress?* I began to write straight from my crooked little heart. Fortunately, there was no shortage of material.

I kept our blog (creatively titled *The Wright Family in Costa Rica*) up to date for months without a hitch, and for the most part people appreciated the new vibe of blunt honesty and the funny, straightforward approach. Of course, not everyone agreed with my thoughts or liked my style or approved of the way that I freely used the entire spectrum of the English language. The price of authenticity in missions became all too clear when, during the worst year of my life (which I promise to tell you about later), I wrote this post:

This Really Happened
(Archive, 10.17.2009)

The other day I was putzing around the house in my PJs, picking up breakfast dishes, sipping coffee, and doing whatever it is I do all day. The boys were at school, Steve was at work, and the house was quiet and still. Just the way I like it. I took my Mac and my coffee to the couch, where I plopped my butt down to get some work done. (We all know that "getting some work done" is code for "aimlessly scrolling Facebook," right?) So I was "working" and sipping and enjoying the quietness and stillness of a new day. And then *this* happened.

As it tends to do when you drink eleven cups of coffee before 9:00 a.m., nature called. And called. And called. Until, at the last possible second, I set my computer aside and sprinted off to, y'know, take a pee. Anyway. I swooped into the bathroom, swiftly dropped my drawers, and took a seat, and when I glanced down, I was shocked to find a pair of black beady eyes looking up at me. *It was a gecko—ON MY THIGH—not three inches from my lady goodies.* Like, apparently this critter had just been chilling out all morning *inside of my pants.*

This really happened!

I. Had a lizard. In my pants.

Of course, I did what any good missionary would do. I wildly smacked at my thigh while I screamed, calling on the name of my Lord and Savior, Jesus (Shit Balls Help Me) Christ, to smite that little bastard and damn it straight to hell. And in case you're wondering, *yes*, this all happened *midpee!*

I'm telling you, if you've never had a midpee emergency, you should count yourself lucky. It took every ounce of control I could muster to remain seated, finish up in a calm and orderly fashion, and retreat quickly back to the living room. That's when I lost it, pacing back and forth like a stark raving madwoman, wheezing and muttering, "I did not sign up for this. I did *not* sign up for this. I did *NOT* sign up for *THIS*."

And then God and I had a little heart-to-heart.

In my hysteria, I let God know quite clearly that I had had *enough*. "I did not sign up," I said, "for lizards in my pants! I didn't sign up for mushrooms growing on my T-shirts. I'm not down with having my butt grabbed by a dude on a bicycle. I am *not okay* with an ant colony living in the sofa. Nope, not okay. And I *especially* did not sign up for having my house robbed, my car stolen, and my credit card used in Vegas. . . . But *this*, God? . . . THIS?? . . . This is the last straw! I cannot live like this. *With lizards in my pants*."

And then I started to ugly cry. Like, really sob, with snot and tears and everything.

"God, are you even there? All I really wanted was to serve you. All I wanted was to honor you and obey your call. All I wanted was for you to *bless* us for being here. *You were supposed to bless us*," I bawled. And then I lay down on the floor and cried out a year's worth of anger and frustration. The hysteria drained out of me, and eventually the tears and snot dried up. You can just imagine the vision of beauty I was by the time it was all over and my house was still and quiet again. Just me and the gecko . . . and God.

I guess I'm not one of those people who learn about God in tidy, conventional ways, like going to church or reading a book. I learn about God when a creepy crawly with suction-cup toes makes it almost all the way from my ankle to the land of milk and honey. And so it took a pervy gecko to help me redefine the way I think of God's blessing.

Listen, I'm not an "audible voice of God" kinda girl. Though I believe it can happen, it never happens to me. But on that morning, while I was wailing like a lunatic, ticking off my laundry list of hardships to the God who'd let me down, I want to say there was the faintest whisper . . . like a breeze, like a breath of air, a response to each of my grievances. *I was with you. . . . I was with you. . . . I was with you. . . .*

I am with you.

And I was reminded of the real blessing of God: that He is with me. He has always been with me. He was with me before I even knew Him.

His presence *is* His blessing—Emanuel— *God is with us.*

About five seconds after I posted that story, one of our supporters called to report me to our sending agency and to tell them she would be withdrawing her fifty-dollar monthly donation. I barely knew her, but she sent me a lengthy e-mail detailing her great disappointment. In her letter, this angry old lady shared that she'd had growing concerns about my "demeanor" for some time, but the breaking point had been the post about the gecko in my pants. In her e-mail the mother of all church ladies said I was "the worst kind of missionary," accusing me of tarnishing the reputation of decent missionaries everywhere, and making good Christians look bad with my filthy mouth and irreverent attitude. She was "appalled" and "dismayed" and she would not support "such blasphemy."

Naturally, I attempted to reply with a humble apology:

> *Dear Mrs. Eatadick,*
> *Thank you for your note. If I understand correctly,*
> *you read about how I found a live critter mere*
> *inches from my vajazzle and you are upset*
> *because I said "shit balls."*
>
> *I would like to say I am so very sorry . . . that*
> *you have no soul.*
>
> *Peace and Love,*
> *Jamie, The Very Worst Missionary*

Which I deleted without sending, because I'm not actually a horrible person.

However disgruntled she was, her complaint did teach me something important: I needed to make a clear distinction between my family's work as missionaries and the personal thoughts and opinions I was tossing out into the universe via the World Wide Web. Good old Mrs. Eatadick's deep convictions inadvertently inspired a complete blog makeover and a whole new title because, the funny thing is, I *agreed* with her. I thought I was a bad missionary too—just not for the same reasons. Delighted by this sweet irony, I redesigned the front page of the blog and dropped ten dollars on my very own domain name to claim the crown and my title as *The Very Worst Missionary.*

Depending on the day, the name of my blog is either a tongue-in-cheek nod to the many Very Good Christians I have managed to offend, or a candid confession from a broken woman doing a crap job at life. But in the end, it's meant to be a question: Is the Very Worst Missionary the one who looks great on the surface, because she does and says all the right things while keeping her secrets secret? Or is the Very Worst Missionary the one who looks like a hot mess on the outside, because her need for redemption is no secret at all?

2

Jew-ISH

My relationship with God has been sort of off and on ever since I was born.

At first, it was more my parents' God, like a great-uncle I'd heard a lot about but never actually met. I knew of God through Old Testament stories, as seen through the eyes of ancient biblical figures like Noah and Jonah and Lot. I thought of God as fierce and strong, in a burning bush, in a pillar of fire, in a den of lions. I thought of God as mean and scary and vengeful, but I was Jewish, so it was cool, because God was on my side.

But this is where it gets kind of weird.

I wasn't actually born Jewish. I was raised *mostly* Jewish by a mostly atheist, antiestablishment, science-fiction-fanatic dad and a mostly agnostic, conflict-avoiding, romance-enthusiast mom. I cannot begin to speculate on what compelled them to walk into a synagogue for the very first time (though I suspect it may

have had something to do with "good business strat-
egy" and a gross stereotype about Jews and money),
as I was merely a baby convert, still in diapers when
my parents made the bold move to Judaism from their
respective Protestant upbringings. All I know is that
they carried my brother and me into a temple, where
the rabbi tucked us safely under his shawl and prayed
us into the family of Abraham. We were only adopted,
of course, but that didn't really matter; from that day
forward I was officially a Jewess.

Committing oneself to a religion is a big decision,
and I have no doubt my parents made their commitment to Judaism with sincerity and purpose. Surely
they did more than just show up at the synagogue one
sunny day and announce their intentions. I know there
must have been classes or some sort of academic or
educational process, because my parents had a ton of
books about being and becoming Jewish. These books
were stacked on the top shelf of their walk-in closet as
far back as I can remember, looking important, collecting dust, and keeping it classy in front of a pile of cheap
romance novels.

As a kid, I loved to read, and I often sneaked into my
parents' room for fresh material. But I never grabbed
any of the hardbound books with words like "Talmud"
or "Torah" along their spines, preferring to reach over
them for tattered paperbacks with names like *Steam-
boat Summer* and *Moonlit Lovers*. Bodice ripper in
hand, I spent countless hours huddled in the closet be-

neath my dad's hanging suit jackets and, above those, *The Laws of Moses.*

We attended synagogue regularly when I was very small, at least for the first few years after our conversion to Judaism. I went to a Jewish day school, had Jewish playmates, recited Hebrew prayers. I have rich memories of celebrating Rosh Hashanah and Yom Kippur, and of lengthy Passover seders with family friends. When I think of these things, I can practically taste the salt water and sweet wine, honey-dipped apples soothing the burn of horseradish on my tongue. We were so Jewish that we dutifully kissed our fingers and touched the mezuzah on the doorpost of our home each time we entered.

As I got older, things changed. My parents had two more kids, and while I don't blame my sisters for my lack of a private school education, it should be noted that my parents enrolled us in public school as soon as they came along. I'm just stating the facts, but whatever. Our big family slowly stopped attending Sabbath services, although we continued to observe the Jewish holidays. I may still have ugly feelings about being forced to play "find the matzo" with Jacob Levi and his cousin Abner over spring break while the lucky Christian kids were eating chocolate bunnies for breakfast and collecting plastic eggs stuffed with jelly beans and two-dollar bills. I loved being Jewish, but secretly I always felt like the Christian holidays were way better for kids.

One December night when I was in third grade, my dad came home from work dragging a big bushy pine tree behind him. He stood it upright in the middle of the living room with one hand, and made a grave declaration that his kids were not gonna grow up without "a goddamn Christmas tree."

Lights and ornaments materialized out of nowhere, and my siblings and I were overjoyed by the shiny red and green balls with delicate hooks and the clean pine scent that quickly filled our home. In retrospect, it must have been a spiritually tumultuous time for my parents, but for the kids it was a nearly storybook evening. My dad was always a bit of an alarmist, so before we nodded off peacefully to visions of sugarplums, he sat us down for a stern warning about the implicit danger of putting lights on trees. And how it kills people. Especially kids. We kissed our parents good night and scampered off to bed with visions of burning houses, screaming children, and wailing mothers who forgot to unplug the goddamn Christmas tree dancing in our heads.

Our surprise first Christmas is a fond childhood memory, but with it came a sudden awareness of two things I found very unsettling. First, I realized faith isn't fixed. It can move. It can morph. It can change. And second? I learned that my parents were . . . *tinsel people.*

That was that. We just sort of stopped being Jewish. No one ever said it out loud; it was never addressed or discussed or explained. The Jewish part of our lives simply *ended*.

Years later, while they were at work, I shamelessly helped myself to whatever private stashes and hidden caches I came across in my parents' bedroom. If I wasn't buried in books at the bottom of their closet while they were out, I was usually digging around in the rest of their bedroom. It was a tween dream come true, as a thorough tossing of drawers revealed a small handgun, a couple of dirty magazines, and a solid year's supply of chewable antacids. But the bottom middle drawer of my parents' dresser was my favorite place to snoop, for that drawer held the only remaining evidence of my Jewish childhood.

There was proof that it all happened. Dreidels my brother and I *literally* made out of clay at Beth Shalom elementary school, a collection of kids' artwork, including my own sloppy preschool attempts to draw the Star of David, and a few pages of my brother's practiced handwritten Hebrew. There were also a couple of carefully folded yarmulkes and a manila folder that held the signed documents that proclaimed us Jewish for real. And wrapped in newspaper at the bottom of it all was the acrylic tortoiseshell menorah we'd gazed upon for so many Hanukkahs, with a handful of bent and broken candles.

When my parents were at work, I would occasionally dig out the menorah and flatten one of the yarmulkes on my head, and then, pulling the little gun from its irresponsible hiding place, I'd run for the mirror in the master bathroom to do some modeling with these exotic props.

Sometimes I would point the gun across the room at an imaginary bad guy, squint my eyes, and launch into what little Hebrew I could remember. I waved the pistol, chanting, *"Barukh ata Adonai,"* like the deranged love child of Clint Eastwood and Yentl. But my very favorite thing to do was hold the gun in one hand, elbow bent at a ninety-degree angle so it was pointed at the ceiling, with the menorah held straight out like an exorcist's crucifix in the other, pretending to be one of Charlie's Angels but, like, *super Jewish.* I looked dangerous yet prayerful, so you couldn't be sure whether I was about to shoot you in the face or bless your ass off.

So anyway. Basically, I lost my religion in the eighties, before R.E.M. even made it a thing. I was Jewish . . . and then I wasn't.

My religious identity just kind of disappeared into thin air. You could say I continued to believed in God throughout my youth, but I also believed in ghosts and unicorns and in that urban legend about a couple making out in a steamy car when an urgent news report alerts them to a one-armed escaped convict in the area, so they buckle up and speed home, only to find a bloody hook dangling from the handle on the car door. I was far too busy crimping my hair, pegging my jeans, and screening my calls with an answering machine to have time to dig deeper for a better understanding of these timeless mysteries.

I never questioned the existence or the purpose of God, but that's only because, as we got less and less Jewish, I never bothered to think about that kind of stuff at all. Just like I never bothered to ask myself why an experienced murderer would open an old-school car door with his clumsy prosthetic hook hand and not his perfectly fine *other* hand. I mean, it doesn't even make sense. But the point is, I didn't care enough to care.

———

I know what you're thinking. You're like, *Why are you telling me this? I thought this book was about a shitty missionary, not some dorky Jewish kid who got a random surprise Christmas. What the hell am I reading?*

Well, I'm telling you this stuff because long before I became the Very Worst Missionary, I was a mostly Jewish gun-waving treasure hunter who lost her religion and didn't really care. I'm telling you all of this because *where you come from matters.*

Your ancestry, your childhood and adolescence, your awful, weird, or wonderful family; it all adds up to who you are today. You can accept or reject the lessons of your youth—your mother's dogma, your father's politics, your ninety-seven-year-old great-granny's super awkward sex advice—but you can't change where you came from, or who you came from, or *what* you came from.

The past lies beneath our beliefs like the soil of our soul. It's the wet clay and dry bones and clumpy dirt, the grit and gravel, the small stones and loose sand, and the petrified turds that the adult formation of our faith must rest upon. Your history is like an inheritance, a patch of land that, though you may not have had much choice in its early cultivation, belongs solely to you.

Fair warning: While I believe it's valuable and necessary, the excavation of your past is a very good way to disrupt your whole entire life as an adult. (I highly recommend the help of a licensed therapist. And possibly medication.) Carefully plucking your way through the landscape of your history can suck, but doing so can help you carry an unsettled faith to solid ground.

It would take a lot of work and a lot of sifting through my own story before I'd understand how my journey as a Christian began long before I actually chose to follow Jesus. I mean, as a little Jewish kid, if you told me I would grow up and someday move to a foreign country as a Christian missionary, I would have laughed in your stupid face. But my mostly Jewish childhood gave me a pretty solid introduction to God while keeping me blessedly far away from churches and churchy people. I was free to learn about Christianity as an adult, without bias or guilt or expectations and, most important, without affection for how things were or how they'd always been. I didn't know it at the time, but making a late entrance to the Christian scene, which at first left me feeling awkward and unsure, would eventually turn out to be an unexpected treasure.

3

Tough

When I was fourteen, I slipped a black leather biker jacket and steel-toed boots over my youth.

I bought them myself with babysitting money, which is kind of a big deal, because in 1989 a reliable babysitter with a reputation for getting the kids to bed on time and doing the dishes could earn a whole two bucks an hour. With a price tag of ninety-nine dollars, it took months of hoarding fives and ones and stacks of quarters in my sock drawer until I finally had enough money for the jacket. It was a broiling 112-degree summer day when I asked my mom for a ride to the mall so I could buy a winter coat, but I was determined to have it. I walked into the leather emporium looking like the girl next door, and I strutted out looking like ... well, the girl next door *in a biker jacket.*

As far as investments go, it was a good one. I wore that jacket every day for at least three years. Plus, it gave me superpowers. When I had it on, I felt invincible. I felt grown up and capable and tough. It allowed me to smoke cigarettes and sip light beer without feeling like a sneaky child. I could flirt, bait, tease, and lie about my age with the greatest of ease, and from the safety of my black leather jacket, I talked to men as if I were a woman. I was only a kid, but when I walked out of my house in that jacket and those boots, with short shorts over black tights and lips the color of red wine, I felt like I could run the world. I could march right into any room, any group, any scenario, and front like a gangster.

Naturally, this got me into a lot of trouble.

I was born with a sharp tongue and the poor taste to say out loud what everyone else is only thinking. The dark-sided Supergirl vibe only gave me more confidence to be an even bigger asshole in public. I could be downright cruel, rude, dismissive, and aloof, the meanest of mean girls, frequently dropping one best friend for another, never getting too close to anyone.

I wanted to be tough, because I thought to be tough was to be unfeeling. I wanted to be made of steel, unbreakable, so I learned to master the swirling mess of fear and insecurity I carried inside. I got so good at hiding it all, so good at pretending nothing bothered me, that when I got drunk and lost my virginity to a complete stranger at a house party, I didn't even bat an eyelash. That night was just confirmation that I possessed control over little in my life, even my own body. But if I could control my emotions, nothing else mattered, because if I didn't let myself feel, then I couldn't be hurt.

Never in the history of the universe has there been a more obvious or pathetic tough-girl facade.

Beyond the lipstick and leather, any reasonable adult could see that I was an incredibly soft, vulnerable child doing her damn best to navigate a chaotic home life and a handful of mental-health issues. The narrow feet stomping around in those big boots were attached to a pretty smart kid with an inexplicable history of academic struggle and a severely underdeveloped sense of self. I wasn't actually a tough girl with a quick wit and a dirty mouth; I was a lost girl with no language for the depression, anxiety, and general disorder that ruled my life.

Unfortunately, as is often the case with teenagers who are off the rails, I suffered a glaring absence in my life of reasonable adults. My parents, bless their hearts, had too many kids, not enough money, and their own bubbling cauldron of undiagnosed mental illnesses between them. I believe they did their best with what they had, and I will always be grateful for their efforts, but my mom and dad were so busy fighting their own demons, I don't really think they could even see mine.

And so I learned to avoid all of the adults who could really see me, instead surrounding myself with those who fed my ugly alter ego. Or rather, fed *on* it. I happily believed my grown-up friends when they told me I was "mature for my age." I assumed they were wise enough to know, but then, my standards for the company I kept were not high. As a high school freshman, I thought hanging out with people who grew pot and made porn and kept a baby possum in a shoebox was cool. It didn't seem at all weird to me that a thirty-five-year-old man was handing out ecstasy like candy and letting a bunch of blitzed teenagers crash at his house every weekend. And while I was quick to pick up on the power of my own sexuality, I remained naive to the fact that grown men who sleep with teenage girls are deviant predators, not "sophisticated older guys." For the longest time I honestly thought *I* was the one manipulating *them*.

I'm grateful I never did anything really, *really* stupid in my black leather jacket and steel-toed boots, like rob a bank or hijack a plane or join a death cult. I'm certain I could have been talked into just about anything, and I'm lucky I didn't end up, like, buried somewhere in the middle of a Mexican desert.

―

During the first semester of tenth grade, the vice principal called me into his office to let me know I'd missed so many classes there was no way I would be able to graduate on time. He said he wanted to understand how a kid who was clever enough to get into honors English could have a GPA that ranked 388 in a class of 390. All I could do was shrug. I really didn't know the answer to that question; I only knew there was something seriously wrong with me. I was fundamentally different from everyone else, but not in a cute, quirky, *Nutty Professor* way, and not in that all-teenagers-think-they're-weird kind of way. I was extraordinarily dysfunctional, though I didn't know why, and I hated myself for it. (It would be another ten years before I'd learn about this thing called ADHD, and twenty before I would seek treatment.)

I didn't tell my parents about my conversation with the vice principal, and to this day I don't know if the school administration ever bothered to call them with news of their daughter's catastrophic failure. Instead, I went home and told my parents that high school didn't stimulate me, I was bored and unmotivated in my studies, and I couldn't bear another day of it. I was ready for college material. It was time for me to move on. I was mature for my age—everyone said so! Then I sold them on the idea of taking the California High School Proficiency Examination so that I could "graduate early" and move forward with my life.

One Saturday that spring, I took a five-hour test, which I passed, and I never set foot in a high school classroom again.

I was fifteen.

And completely untethered.

There was nowhere I needed to be and no one I needed to be with. I had no real God; I observed no moral code; I knew no intrinsic worth. I lived the next few years of my life almost like a body without a spirit. I couldn't be hurt or disappointed. I couldn't be victimized or violated. I pretended to be emotionally bankrupt; that way the vault was empty—even if someone violently broke in, there was nothing for them to take. This lent a false sense of protection as I engaged in more and more risky behavior. I was extremely promiscuous. I dabbled in drugs. I jumped in cars with all the wrong people and took off my clothes for all the wrong reasons.

Still too young to get a driver's license, I rolled up for my first day of community college in the passenger seat of my mom's minivan. Initially, I enrolled in super easy classes like Psych 101, Bonehead Math, and Intro to Fencing. The next semester I tried to expand my horizons. I took a writing class (which I dropped immediately, because writing is *so much work*. No, thank you!), but I was surprised to fall in love with the nuances of anthropology and the broad impact of world history.

I'd like to tell you this was a major turning point for me, like I suddenly discovered the joy of learning and a hidden capacity for getting shit done, and then I kicked ass in college. But there was no reason the academic struggles I'd had since kindergarten wouldn't follow me on this new journey. The truth is, nothing changed. The only difference was that now I could drop classes before my disastrous habits were immortalized on my transcripts. Also, college professors wouldn't write concerned notes to my parents that said things like "Jamie is a bright girl with great potential, but she often arrives unprepared, spends class time daydreaming, and never turns in her work."

Sadly, failing out of high school wasn't the rock-bottom event it should have been. "Graduating early" and going to college only furthered the delusion that I was somehow taking charge of my life. I convinced myself I'd chosen that path on purpose, ignoring the part where I'd backed myself into a corner and run out of options. I never told anyone that I quit high school before high school quit me, and it was easy to let college classmates and professors believe I was there because I was extra smart, not because I was actually *really dumb*. Despite the fact that I'd literally failed my way there, when I walked around the American River Community College campus in my black leather jacket and chunky combat boots, I felt like a total badass.

But mostly I was just an ass.

———

I like to think I grew up to be the kind of reasonable adult I so badly needed entering my teen years. Personal experience has given me eyes for seeing beyond the icy exterior of the troubled kid who's hiding a hurricane of pain. I cringe when I see girls who remind me of me, for I certainly have regrets from that period of my life, but I'm also filled with understanding and compassion for them. I would scoop them up and hug them and tell them they're enough, if I thought it would actually spare them a few years' worth of embarrassing behavior.

But of all the stupid, dangerous, disgusting things

I did in my youth, I carry a deep, abiding shame over only one thing—and it's *not* that I was a gullible, drunk slut; it's that I didn't complete four years of high school. I mean, it's one thing to be a dumb kid with poor judgment, but even the biggest burnout potheads I knew made it all the way through their senior year, walked the stage in a cap and gown, and went home with a diploma. I've known some people with college degrees, master's degrees, even a couple of PhDs who function at, like, borderline chimpanzee-level intelligence, but I couldn't even manage *high school.*

I'm still trying to make peace with that silly child who daydreamed her life away. I'm still kind of pissed at the girl who was always unprepared, still disappointed in the one who didn't do her work and frustrated by her inability to get her shit together. I'm annoyed with the girl who made a mess of her life and then pretended the only way out of the mess she'd created was exactly the way she wanted to go, as if it had been her plan all along. That girl? The one with so much "potential"? . . . Ugh. I just want to kick her.

Probably because I still am her.

When you struggle in your forties with things that wrecked you at fifteen, I don't think you're supposed to say so out loud. It makes people uncomfortable.

Everyone loves an underdog, but we prefer our stories of wrestling and redemption to be told in the past tense: I *was* depressed. I *had* anxiety. I *felt* insecure. I *slept* around. Our favorite books, movies, and heroes offer us inspirational retrospectives of overcoming and winning—we're all about killing the monster. We'd rather hear from our drunks when they're sober, our depressed when they're happy, our sick when they're healed. We want to see wild horses broken and to believe in the hands that tamed them, because most of us hold our own dark places of wrestling with unbridled messes in our souls that sometimes spill over into life, and we desperately need to see that maybe we too can overcome the things that are ruining us.

But I'm afraid I've invited you into a story that hasn't yet reached its redemptive conclusion. As much as I'd love to spin a tale that wraps up nicely with a great big bow, this one does not. For I still *have* depression and anxiety. I *feel* insecure. I *am* dysfunctional. (For the record, I *do not* sleep around.)

I can tell you that, as I've walked along with God, I've experienced growth and development in areas I never thought possible. I've received forgiveness for things I once thought unforgivable. I've been healed of emotional wounds that might have killed me, had I never come to know this love. But—spoiler alert!—a life of faith is not the happy, clappy Valtrex commercial some would have you believe. God will not be swallowed like a pill to cure the herpes of your soul so you can run in a field of sunflowers with your hot boyfriend.

It just doesn't go down like that. No matter how much we beg and plead, nor how fervently we pray, having faith does not release us from the hard work of maturing.

It's true, I'm not the girl next door hiding in a biker jacket anymore. . . . I'm a grown-ass woman in a biker jacket, thank you very much. These days I feel nothing but mercy for the girl I used to be—the party girl who once snorted coke off the back of a toilet, the naive teenager who couldn't see that her much older "boyfriend" was actually a creepy pedophile, the scrappy little jackass who got in a fistfight, in a restaurant, *over a salad* . . . that girl needed love, and by God's grace, I've learned to love her.

And even in my forties I've found that a brazen little girl's badassery is useful from time to time.

4

A Butt-Hair-Milkshake Love Story

If Brett Williams hadn't sprinkled butt hair in my milkshake, we wouldn't even be having this conversation.

I would be some other Jamie, with some other husband, and some other kids, and some other memories, and you'd be reading some other book, because these stories would not have taken life and these pages would never have been written. This is *all* because of a handful of butt hairs, casually tossed into a chocolate milkshake amid the repressed snorts and giggles of the punk-ass teenage pranksters I called friends.

I am dead serious.

While I was in the bathroom, Brett Williams threw butt hairs in my unguarded milkshake, and, as far as I know, I swallowed at least some of them, and *then everything changed forever.* (So here's an important piece of advice: If you are a juvenile delinquent hanging out in a twenty-four-hour diner after midnight on a weekday and you need to use the restroom, *do not* trust your uneaten food to your friends, especially if your friends are a bunch of assholes, because there's a good chance it will be tampered with in your absence and you'll end up ingesting something you'd rather not. Like hot sauce. Or coffee creamer. *Or butt hair.* And your life will never be the same.)

I should have trusted my instincts that night, because I knew something was weird as soon as I got back from the bathroom. The table was too quiet and my friends were practically humming with the electric buzz of anticipation. Watching them watch me, I dragged the tall frosty glass to the edge of the table, leaned over it, and, highly suspicious of the expectant looks on their ugly faces, I dove into that shake like my life depended on it. I drank deeply, with a rebellious flair, to show them I knew they'd done *something* but I was made of iron. Nothing would make me flinch. Before the straw left my lips, the group erupted in peals of laughter, howls of disgust, and breathless declarations, "Ohmygawd! Ohmygawd! *You drank it! You drank it!* Brett put *butt hair* in your shake and *you drank it!*"

A half dozen stupid fingers pointed from me to the shake to the bald spot on Brett's hairy butt cheek, and all around me stupid mouths gaped open on stupid red faces, as my friends' stupid bodies shook and twisted and quaked with mirth. There is no feeling in the world quite like the disturbing loneliness that comes with being the butt of a really good joke, and I've gotta admit, as a well-practiced bully I wasn't used to it. It threw me off my game. Typically I'd have been ready with a biting remark or a snarky comeback, but *I'd just eaten butt hair*, so my brain was busy trying to kill itself. I stood up and stared back in uncharacteristic silence at the group of kids writhing in laughter at my expense, and I wished them all dead.

Adulthood taught me how to own the feeling of embarrassment, how to rock even the most awkward moment with a measure of grace, how to walk away with my head held high, dignity intact—or, at least, now I know how to fake it. But as a sixteen-year-old girl, overly defensive and totally insecure, my face burned with humiliation and my guts boiled over with rage. I wanted to barf, because *butt hair*, but I also wanted to cry, to scream, to hide, to break a bottle and cut somebody.

I did not want to laugh. I did not want to "be cool" or "chill out" or "relax."

Certain I would never live down my new reputation as the girl who ate ass fur, I thought my best option was probably to set the restaurant on fire and flee to rural Arkansas, where I could live in the woods and be friends with squirrels and never make eye contact with another human being ever again. The only thing stopping me was that I didn't have a lighter on me. Or a ride to Arkansas. And I'd just spent my last four dollars on a chocolate shake I would never enjoy.

When it was time to leave, I refused to get in the car with Brett, who was both the violator of my midnight snack and my middle-of-the-night ride home. Without a word, I walked past my usual spot in the front seat of Brett's piece-of-crap Honda Civic and kept going toward the car parked directly across from it. I crossed through the narrow space in the glaring headlights between bumpers, making my way to the empty passenger side of a slightly less shitty Nissan Sentra, where I opened the door and climbed in, uninvited. Smiling over the dash, I waved a smug good-bye to Brett Williams—*Do not mess with my milkshake, asshole!*—and kicked him right in the teen crush.

Although we'd never hung out just the two of us, I'd been friends with the tall, broad, grinning football player in the driver's seat next to me for a few months before "the incident." It's fair to say we were both surprised when I jumped into his car and turned a flirty face toward him for a favor, but *no one* would have guessed that I'd just asked the boy I would marry for a ride home.

That fateful night, I gave my number to Steve, the tall guy in the little sedan, and we started to write a love story the way teenagers did in the nineties; by talking on the phone for ten consecutive hours, doing it in the car, and listening to the Cure on an endless loop. After six months of dating like this, we did *the most embarrassing thing ever* and got teenage engaged. (I swear, there is nothing funnier than a teenage girl talking about her "fiancé.") We genuinely believed that we were in love, but, to be honest, I don't think our relationship would have lasted very long if things had gone differently. He lived an hour away at college, we saw each other only on weekends, and the truth is, we didn't really have much in common outside of car sex and the Cure. We were probably on the brink of a classic adolescent breakup when, a few months after he put a ring on it, he put a fetus in it.

Whoops.

All in all, it was a year and a half between the life-altering moment at the diner and the earth-shattering second of my baby's first breath. Eighteen months from milkshake to motherhood.

———

Screwing up my own life over and over again was one thing, but dropping a baby-sized bomb in the middle of someone else's path was a startling expansion of my destructive capacity. I couldn't ruin this guy's life, could I? Though Steve's reaction to the possibility of a pregnancy was kind and supportive, I didn't think I could do it. I couldn't have a baby. . . . I couldn't even keep my room clean.

For my first-ever visit to a gynecologist, I took great pains to prepare, showering, shaving, y'know, just generally sprucing things up. I mean, a few people had been down there before, but never a *professional*, and I didn't want my doctor to think I was some kind of amateur. Despite my best efforts to play it cool, the office staff could tell right away that I was a newbie, so they guided me carefully through each step of the awkwardness. Sign in here. Put your cup of pee there. Wear the gown like this. They were comforting and kind and almost motherly, and I thought, *They are gonna be so happy for me when we all find out I'm not pregnant and this is just a big misunderstanding.*

After I put on the requisite blue gown, open at the front as instructed, I sat on the paper-covered exam table and waited. While I waited, I reminded myself that those cheap grocery-store pregnancy tests are wrong, like, *all the time*, and I made a mental note that since I was already at the doctor's office, I should definitely ask about birth control. There was a quick rap on the door before it swung open, and I nearly fell off the table. I knew I had a Latin American doctor, but I was not expecting Enrique Iglesias in a lab coat to glide in with a smile brighter than the sun, shake my hand, and blurt out, "Congratulations, you're pregnant!"

I was speechless, still trying to get my head around the doctor's blunt but definitive announcement (and also his beautiful brown angel face), when he asked me to lie back so he could get an idea of just how pregnant I was. Dr. Guapo took one look at my abdomen and said, "Wow, look at that cantaloupe!" and I lifted my head to see what I'd been ignoring for so long. Where there should have been a smooth flat plain between two visible hip bones, there was the soft round beginning of a baby bump. An ultrasound confirmed what the doctor accurately guessed with a little bit of prodding and a measuring tape—I was sixteen weeks along.

Six. Teen. Weeks.

That's second-trimester pregnant.

That's time-for-stretchy-pants pregnant.

That's just-a-few-months-until-you're-not-pregnant
-anymore pregnant.

I would walk out of the office that day with a long
strip of ultrasound pictures that smelled like ink and
held, in fuzzy black-and-white images, a challenging
contrast to the girl who'd worked so hard for so long to
feel dead inside. Beautiful, terrifying, and utterly undeniable, there it was. *Proof of life.*

The moment I saw my itty-bitty bean of a baby wig-
gling around in a cozy home perched right above my
bladder—that perfect little profile, the zipper curve of a
spine, minuscule fingers and toes, and a heartbeat that
flashed like Morse code to my soul—I knew I would
never be the same. I'd been living a mannequin's existence: hollow, fake, unfeeling. I'd emptied myself out
to protect myself from pain. Suddenly I had a purpose
and a future that required not just my physical presence but my heartfelt participation. I'd accidentally
made a tiny person, and I probably should have been
scared to death, but through the sonar *whoosh whoosh
whoosh* of our heartbeats weaving together in the exam
room, we shared an unspoken promise: I would bring
that baby into the world, and that baby would bring
me to life.

I shed my identity as a tough girl, trading in the black
leather jacket and steel-toed boots for an overstuffed
diaper bag and a poorly fitted wedding dress. Since

I was only seventeen, it seemed especially important that I act, speak, and look like a responsible adult if I wanted to be taken seriously as a mother. Fortunately, in 1993 mom jeans were the only jeans, so the look wasn't hard to pull off, but I'd have to fake my way through the other stuff. I got my driver's license, dropped all of my community-college classes, and picked up a decent full-time job working swing shifts at a twenty-four-hour call center.

For reasons that made perfect sense at the time, Steve and I decided to wait until after the baby was born to get married. We didn't want people to think we were getting married *just because* I was knocked up. We didn't want to rush things *just because* there was an actual human baby on the way. We didn't want to feel like we *had* to get married *just because* all of our parents, grandparents, aunts, uncles, cousins, brothers, sisters, neighbors, and strangers expected us to. We were practically almost grown-ups, dammit, and we wanted to do things *our way*.

While I was pregnant, I would live in my parents' house, work for as long as possible, and save every penny in preparation for our family. Steve would stay in his dorm on campus, an hour away, and complete his sophomore year as an engineering major on a full-ride athletic scholarship. The timing was good, because the baby was due in February, after football season, and we could get married in May, after finals. Our plan would give us a financial head start before the kid came, plus some time to arrange for a little wedding.

It was the most sensible way to move forward, but it left me largely alone to walk through pregnancy and prepare for a baby, while Steve's life carried on virtually unchanged. He went to classes (when he felt like it), ate cafeteria food, worked out, weight-trained, went to practice, watched football film, drank cheap beer, and hung out with his friends. On weekends during the football season, I rode to home games with his parents and waited anxiously afterward for him to emerge from the locker room, bruised, swollen, exhausted, and—if his team lost—*pissed*. If there was an away game, he traveled by chartered plane or tour bus, played his heart out, and then was free to drink himself into oblivion.

Mostly I worked and slept and ate. I went to doctor appointments alone and then shared any news with Steve during a nightly phone call, telling him how big my expanding belly measured and reporting any lab results or interesting tidbits about fetal development. At my twenty-week appointment, I learned our baby's gender and rushed home to wait by the phone, willing Steve to call me from the pay phone in his dorm so I could tell him his wish had been granted: We were having a boy.

He was so excited, he dropped the receiver and started running up and down the busy hall, shouting and cheering, "It's a boy! It's a boy! I have a son!" to a reception of hugs and handshakes and hearty congratulations. While the revelry went on, I sat in the dark on the floor in my childhood bedroom with the phone pressed hard against my ear, listening and smiling, relieved by his overwhelming joy and thankful for the celebration happening on the other end of the line. I would wait until after we hung up to break down sobbing.

I couldn't shake the feeling that I was only ever supposed to be a temporary stop for Steve, the bad girl on his way to happily ever after with some basic sorority bitch. Obviously, we were equally responsible for this unplanned pregnancy, and together we had agreed to keep our baby, but in my eyes Steve was a golden boy who could do no wrong, and I was the go-nowhere loser who would only hold him back.

———

On a chilly Tuesday morning in February, with my fiancé (LOL) by my side, that baby and I made good on our promise to each other. I delivered him into the world, and he thrust me into a love so deep and so pure, it set my soul on fire.

With my son's birth came my first real glimpse of God, and I don't mean in the "miracle of life" kind of way. I mean that when I held my infant's body against my chest, when I smelled his downy head and let his fingers curl around my thumb, when I stared at his perfectly pursed lips, I could see God at work. I could see clearly how blessings are sometimes born of bad circumstances, how happiness can come through heartbreak, how peace and discord can walk hand in hand,

and how a messed-up seventeen-year-old who can't even keep her own room clean can still do great things.

In his tiny face I saw a bigger picture.

I watched my little bundle of boy with awe and wonder for hours, filled with a fierce, abiding love and a fresh new fear of the future. I still wasn't sure if I could do it—raise this child, be his mom, nurture him and protect him and guide him. I felt honored but so afraid, and familiar feelings of inadequacy came creeping back in to convince me I was in over my head. Then the baby, *my baby*—the first person I had willingly suffered and sacrificed for, the one I would easily die for— arched his soft back to stretch his squishy little body. He opened a pair of dark eyes to take in the world and he started to whimper, because when you are naked and small the world is big and scary. When I spoke softly to my infant son, he calmed at the sound of his mama's voice, and just like that, to one person, mine had become the voice of comfort and authority. And it was as if God Himself leaned in to whisper, *Look what you can do.*

5

I'm Not Done

At six feet six inches and 280 pounds, my young husband-to-be was a monster of a man. He had a baby face over broad shoulders and a sloping back, with lats that pushed his arms out and away from his sides when he walked. His thighs were so big he had to cut the seams on the leg holes of his boxers to make them fit, and when he stood next to me, it made me feel petite in that lame, cutesy, girly kind of way, and *I loved it*.

Steve made sort of a Neanderthal first impression, but he was actually smart. Like, *super smart.* He was the only athlete who lived in the freshman honors dorm, and he loved all kinds of nerdy shit like advanced math and building computers and playing board games. To be honest, he was so smart that sometimes he made me feel dumb, and I didn't love that—but I actually didn't hate it either, because I loved being loved by such a smart guy.

I thought Steve hung the moon and the stars, and I

found great satisfaction in simply being *his*. It sounds so syrupy and gross when I say it like that, but it's true. I felt validated by his awesomeness. With no real accomplishments of my own, I could cling to his, as if they somehow reflected my own capacity for greatness. I happily forged much of my identity from scraps of Steve's life, believing, deep down, that I was only as good as the best person who loved me.

And so I wanted nothing more than to be "Steve's wife" forever.

Just before I walked down the aisle to marry him, I slipped into a dimly lit bathroom for one last look in the mirror. I checked my makeup and twirled a loose strand of hair into a curl, adjusting the plastic comb that held a long ivory veil at the back of my head. My dress was kind of wonky, since I'd made the mistake of buying it from a clearance warehouse in San Francisco's garment district about three weeks after I'd given birth. It could be taken in only so much, so on my wedding day I stuffed my bra with two pairs of socks, straightened the loose fabric that rippled around my rib cage, and called it good.

This was it. In ten minutes I would marry my four-month-old baby's daddy and the best guy I'd ever dated. I couldn't believe how lucky I was that it was Steve. I mean, I could have gotten knocked up by any one of the many dirtbag loser alcoholic wannabe rock stars I'd slept with, and been stuck with that guy forever. But somehow I'd lucked out and gotten stuck with Steve. At that very moment, my great big small-town boy was waiting for me to meet him at the altar, so I pushed every guy who'd come before him out of my head and offered myself a congratulatory smile. It was a tiny acknowledgment of triumph on my wedding day, like a cosmic wink to say, *Girl, you dodged a bullet.*

When the wedding song played, I made my way to the front of the church, where I promised my heart and my soul and the rest of my life to the nervous man-child sweating in a rented tux by my side. With tears in our eyes, we stood face to face, hand in hand, and repeated our vows to each other. It was all the standard stuff—the traditional better or worse, richer or poorer, sickness or health, until somebody kicks the bucket, followed by an exchange of rings and a quick prayer. We sealed the deal with a kiss, which had the loud, smacking quality of a child kissing their grandma on the lips. It wasn't sweet or romantic or even jubilant; it was just *awkward.*

As the short ceremony came to a close, someone handed us our baby in his own tiny tuxedo, and the college football team chaplain pronounced us "Mr. and Mrs. Wright" for the very first time. I will never forget looking up at my brand-new husband in the soft golden light of the church and feeling like I had to be the luckiest girl who ever lived. And honestly, I probably did dodge a bullet on my wedding day . . . but I stepped on a land mine.

Barely an adult, Steve was in no way prepared for marriage or fatherhood. It took him about five minutes to resent having a wife around all the time, and he found the baby's constant needs bothersome. But worse, my easy, unconditional love for our infant son jabbed at a deep-seated insecurity in Steve. He didn't want to share his wife's affection, not even with his own child, and his resentment was obvious to pretty much everyone but me.

I worked full time, took care of our little guy, and dutifully made excuses for Steve's extreme mood swings and simmering rage. He was tired; he had a lot on his plate; he was stressed from school and sore from football. On the nights the anger radiated in waves off my new husband's broad back as he turned away from me in bed, I allowed myself to believe I deserved it. I'd let the laundry pile up and the kitchen was a mess. I'd forgotten to call the plumber. I'd spent too much on groceries. It was, quite frankly, easier for me to carry the burden of his emotional issues than it was for me to admit that maybe marrying him had been a huge mistake.

I'm still not sure if I was unable or just unwilling to see it, but it would take me years to finally accept that Steve was not the perfect man I'd unfairly made him out to be.

The thing is, I really needed Steve to be a good person, because I thought that made me good. My self-worth was so dependent upon him being a great guy that I ignored the kinds of red flags that would have sent any self-respecting woman running as fast as if her own ass were on fire. But I wasn't self-respecting, I was Steve-revering, which in the long run wouldn't prove healthy or helpful for either of us.

I remained blind to his character flaws for years, blissfully ignorant of his brokenness and consequently of the depth of brokenness in my own marriage. But that's not to say either of us spent time pretending to be deliriously happy. We found plenty of shit to fight about.

The first time we decided to get a divorce was just a few months after our first anniversary. I can't remember if the argument started over the laundry or the dishes or money or parenting or what to watch on TV or where to get takeout or who ate the last of the ice cream, but it was definitely one of those things. What started it doesn't even matter; we needed only a tiny strike to spark the bonfire of bitterness and resentment between us, a blazing circle of accusations and indignation that continued to burn hot until one of us finally announced we were done. Done. That's what you say when you decide to get a divorce. You say, "You know what? I'm done."

Or if you're really, really serious, you say, "That's it! *We are done.*" I was done with his antics and he was done with my garbage and we were *just . . . so . . . done.*

Our fight that day was huge, and we both played the "done" card, but I had an office party that night, and we'd already spent $80 on tickets (which was like

$450 to us at the time). Once things calmed down, the babysitter was on her way over, and rather than send her home, we decided to go ahead and go to the stupid party. We agreed this would be our last night out as a couple, and then tomorrow? *We were so totally done.*

It was a theme party, a luau, with a giant pig roasting in the ground and hula dancers and Polynesian drummers and everything. Everyone was dressed accordingly in Hawaiian shirts and puka-shell necklaces and tropical-print dresses with leis. As far as office parties go, it was a pretty good one, but it was still an office party—180 coworkers who knew one another only through weekday small talk, now making even smaller small talk with their coworkers' spouses.

We had driven to the party in silence, putting on fake smiles as we found our assigned table and greeted a few of the other guests. We were there to make good on our eighty-dollar investment and to give our poor toddler a break from his angry, stressed-out parents, but we had no intention of having any fun at all. Since small talk with strangers is the most horrible kind of torture, it seemed like having a terrible time would be easy. The problem is? Steve and I are just kinda fun together. We can't even help it.

We usually like the same food and hate the same people, so a catered party with a roasted pig and a tableful of goobers we'd just met was, like, the perfect combination to make us both wonder if maybe we weren't done after all. You simply can't moan in ecstasy with someone over the sheer deliciousness of a certain appetizer and not wonder if you need to spend the rest of your life together. And you can't squeeze someone's thigh under the tablecloth when your department head's husband takes off his shoes to show you his bunions without thinking about how maybe, *just maybe*, you'd be better off growing old with that thigh nearby. These feelings were undeniable, and we slowly began to emerge from the fog of our big fight.

But it was the hula-hoop contest that saved our marriage that day. Neither of us is all that great at hula hoop, so our chances of winning were slim, but there were prizes, and we both love prizes, so we signed up for the "most creative" category and hatched a plan. When the spotlight landed on us, I hiked up my cocktail dress, and Steve lifted me up over his head to straddle his shoulders. Together we stood like a totem pole made of white people, and I twirled three hula hoops around my neck while my giant of a husband spread his arms wide, *Christ the Redeemer* style, throwing shade all over the competition with his massive wingspan.

The crowd went wild!

We took home the grand prize that night: a blue plastic pitcher with a set of four matching tumblers on a serving tray covered in sea horses.

We won.

And we weren't done.

See, the problem is, Steve and I were pretty much made for each other.

I don't mean that in a soul-mates kind of way, unless by "soul mates" you mean people whose psychological disorders play exceptionally well together. You know, like when a girl who uses sex to feel loved falls in love with a guy who uses sex to feel numb. Or when a guy who strives for success in order to feel valued falls in love with a girl who finds her value in supporting his success. This is how, between us, we carried a psych ward's worth of dysfunction into our marriage. At the time, I had no idea that buried underneath his accomplished exterior, Steve was just as broken and scared and sad and hurting as me. In the decades ahead, I would come to understand that, while my insecurity turned inward in the form of self-loathing and the core belief that I was undeserving of love, his insecurity turned outward. He searched for validation by performing for affirmation, believing that love was a competition to be won and that he could be loved only if and when he earned it.

Basically, we were a walking marriage crisis.

But we were also babies with a baby. We had a family, and bills, and chores, and sports, and friends, and work parties; busy lives that helped us to forget that just under the surface everything was not as it should be. And while we were really bad for each other—like, possibly the *absolute worst* for each other—we genuinely loved each other in our own silly, broken ways.

It's nothing short of a miracle that our marriage survived and has continued to survive for more than twenty-three years, day by day. Sometimes minute by minute. Sometimes one hula-hoop contest at a time.

———

Who would have imagined that someday that same train wreck of a couple would end up as Christian missionaries in Costa Rica? Certainly not us. And definitely no one who knew us. But it was, at least in part, the difficulty of marriage that set our souls to searching for something . . . I don't know . . . *more*.

I warned you this is not a finished story; it's a messy work of redemption, a peek into real life in progress. Thankfully, we've both developed into quite different people since those rocky early years, mostly thanks to a great many hours of therapy. But we'll probably have to fight off the lies in our heads until the day we die. Even when we're old, we'll still be doing the daily work of growing up.

Marriage is just so fucking hard, and we're all looking for someone to tell us it won't always be. We want someone to encourage us to hang in there with a promise that it gets better. And maybe right now you're as desperate as I have been at times for someone to tell you that the deep, dark issues lurking behind your closed doors can be prayed away, easy as pie, and your life and your partner and your heart will be restored, as good as new. But I'm not gonna lie to you. The truth is marriage is a shit ton of work, and as far as I know, it never stops being hard.

Wow. Can you tell I'm in a really bad mood right now? *Someone* kept stealing all the covers last night.

Anyway, if there is a formula for the perfect relationship, I certainly don't know it, but I can tell you this: I fought for my marriage for many, many years before I realized I'd been fighting the wrong battle entirely. I was fighting to be loved and to be wanted and to be worthy in the only way I knew how, which was by fighting to be Steve's wife, when I should have been fighting to be *me*. Early on, I didn't understand that the best thing I could have done for my husband, for myself, and for our marriage would have been to show us both that I am my own person. I make my own contributions to the world, I carry my own significance, and I am infinitely loved by a good God.

So I am good, not because of Steve or despite him but entirely apart from him.

And I'm not done.

PART 2

An Unconventional Faith

6

Good Christian

The first time I walked into a church, I might as well have had a red bull's-eye painted directly over my heart. You couldn't have picked a more perfect walking target for somebody's next "intentional relationship." I was scared and sad and deeply wounded, and I was looking for someone to tell me that life would be okay.

One Sunday morning when Steve wasn't home, I made my way to the church closest to our house, nervously checked my little boy into the kids' program, and sat alone in the very last row, as near to the exit I could possibly get. I was there not out of curiosity or even genuine interest but out of sheer desperation.

Growing up, I'd heard over and over again that Christians are losers who don't know how to live their own lives. I was told Christians are pathetic dummies who need a crutch to lean on because they can't stand on their own two feet. I was taught to see Jesus as a leader for people who couldn't think for themselves and needed to be told what to do. So as a confused nineteen-year-old with a child I didn't know how to raise, a husband I didn't know how to love, and a life I had no idea how to live, it seemed like maybe I should meet this Jesus, the God of pitiful weaklings who are limping along without a clue.

Turns out they were right. Jesus was exactly who I needed.

Much to my surprise, I found a sense of belonging in church and unexpected joy in the pursuit of faith. In those early days I was like a rescue puppy: precious and needy, dying for love and affection, begging for reassurance. I was ready and willing to be trained by the first family who would take me home, and that family was the church. I lapped up their attention and they were kind and gentle and gracious, teaching me the rules and showing me how to behave, and for a while I was content to simply perform.

Sit. Stay. *Good Christian.*

As a straight, white, middle-class stay-at-home mom, I was an ideal fit for the suburban church. I mean, it was almost like the church was made for someone just like me. The music was catchy, and the band played long enough to accommodate late arrivals. Sermons were short and sweet, and the offering was timed perfectly so that checks could be written and stuffed into envelopes before the basket passed by. The children's program was perfectly safe and spotlessly clean, with rooms segregated by age and decorated in adorable kid-friendly versions of terrifying Old Testament stories: Noah's ark, David and Goliath, and Jonah and his chubby pet whale. *So cute.* Overall, the church experience was organized and comfortable and free from distractions—which happened to be *exactly* what I wanted for an hour every Sunday. Oh, and there was coffee!

It took me a little while to learn the special language and the secret codes of churchiness, and some things took a little bit longer to figure out than others. Like, when the worship leader cried, "Lift your voice!" did he mean my *actual voice*? Because I was 95 percent certain no one else was singing. The music was so loud it was impossible to tell for sure, but I could have sworn they were just moving their mouths. So I compromised, mouthing the words with lightly audible vowels and just a whisper of an *S* every now and then. (For the record, this is still how I sing in church.) Fortunately, I was quicker to pick up on other things. Proper Sunday attire, for example, meant basically nothing too slutty and nothing you borrowed from a homeless person. Of course, that unspoken rule was easy to grasp, because everyone knows that the church is no place for whores and hobos.

Church was like a club, and the rules of the club were simple: Dress this way. Use these words, but *do not* use *those* words. Go here on Sunday morning and there on Wednesday night. Be appalled by this, and this, and that, and them (but especially *them*). Get indignant about so-and-so and offended by such-and-such. And, above all, act like everything is okay (even if it's definitely not), because you have Jesus and Jesus makes life pretty. The good Christians conformed to these rules without question, and when they talked about maturing in their faith, it seemed like what they meant was obeying the rules with more consistency and breaking the rules less often. To *sit* and *stay* was their endgame, and I thought it was supposed to be mine.

I was in it for the long haul.

The only thing that could have made this foray into the church world better would have been if Steve had been in it with me. By then his job as a sheriff's deputy had him working every Sunday, so I was on my own as far as church was concerned. I could go or not go; he didn't really care either way. . . . Ha, just kidding! Steve was *super pissed* when I started going to church. In fact, he *forbade me* to give the church money, being sure to let me know he thought it was all brainwashing, bullshit, and propaganda. I couldn't really blame him. He'd grown up heavily involved in a local church but walked away in his teens after a married pastor ran off with a married congregant, leaving two devastated families and a stunned congregation in their wake. Years later, Steve was still pretty bitter about it, but his distaste for organized religion didn't do a thing to discourage my weekly church attendance.

I respected Steve's opinion, but Jesus was blowing my mind. And to be honest? I *loved* being in the club. Despite my husband's ever-rolling eyes, I did everything I could to look and sound like the good Christians did. I tuned my car radio to the Fish, hung a little gold cross around my neck, and I even cut my hair into a classic Christian mom bob so people would know at a glance that I was in the club. Whenever possible, I used my new Christian vocabulary. I wasn't lucky or wealthy or healthy anymore; I was *blessed*. I didn't hang out with people; I had *fellowship* with them. If someone lost their job, it wasn't because of company-wide layoffs or because they were just a shitty employee; it was the hand of God *closing one door to open another*.

Once, in an effort to use, like, every single Christian word I'd ever heard, I took my baby sister to Carl's Jr. to evangelize her over Western Bacon Cheeseburgers and onion rings. She was like thirteen, and I told her all about sin and sanctification and redemption and resurrection and how she too could have a place in heaven for all of eternity. When she got up to use the restroom (probably hoping to escape through an open window), the old ladies in the booth next to me leaned over to pat me on the back and tell me I was doing a good job. They were obviously in the club and had recognized me by my words. Or maybe by my hair.

Anyway. I intentionally relationshipped my sister so hard that day, she didn't really want to hang out with me after that. I might have considered that perhaps it was my gross evangelism tactics that had pushed her away, but I didn't. I just assumed she was busy, congratulated myself for *planting seeds*, and went on with my life.

———

Man, those were the glory days—back when Sunday sermons were fill-in-the-blanks, everybody ate muffins and scones at weekly Bible studies, and following Jesus seemed as simple as following the rules. But then gluten intolerance and intolerable Christians went and ruined all the fun.

My attempt to conform to the good Christian way was genuine and heartfelt, but later I would come to realize that I hadn't actually *become* a good Christian at all. I was just really good at looking like one.

I'd spent my whole life pretending to be someone I wasn't so that I would be safe, accepted, popular, worthy, wanted, and loved. Walking into church was no different. Except it was worse. Because if you slip out of character and go against secular social norms, people just think you're weird, but when you push against the church order, people in the club think you're *bad*. And they call you names behind your back, like "dangerous."

I was doing all the good Christian things and obeying all of the good Christian rules, and just when I thought I *finally* had the whole church thing figured out . . . Jesus swooped in and fucked everything up.

The questions started during a study of the life of Christ, because that was the first time I truly looked beyond how everyone else was doing it and started to see how Jesus did it. I began to really *see* what he said and where he went and what he did and how he treated people. The guy touched lepers with his bare hands and hung out with the neighborhood undesirables. He talked to the impoverished, the infirm, the outcast as though they mattered as much as anybody. And when faced with greed and corruption in a house of God, Jesus braided a whip and quite literally overturned the tables of injustice. When I took the time to examine how he lived out his days on earth, it changed everything about how I saw the club. Following Jesus started to make a lot more sense—but the *church* started to look kinda wonky.

For the first few years, I kept quiet, though. In the club, you don't express dissent. I didn't want to be seen as immature or unfaithful, disruptive or dangerous. Why would anyone in the clubhouse want to look like a bad Christian?

Inherently I just knew that to question the system was a violation of some unspoken law. But secretly I was also dying to know if anyone else was giving a proper side-eye to some of the stuff we were doing and saying.

Like, did anyone else notice that you can follow *all* of the good Christian rules and still be a huge dick about it? Seriously. I can say things right to your face that'll make you want to slit your wrists, and I can do it with church-approved language, dripping with sweetness and an air of concern. I can lead you to believe God hates your guts and I can make you wish you were never born while I claim to "speak the truth in love," promising that I only want what's best for you.

I wondered if others were plagued by the same nagging feeling that Jesus would probably be going to church with the whores and the hobos.

It was only a theory, as I was still pretty new to this Christianity thing, but I suspected that Jesus might have leaned more toward meeting the felt needs of the poor and the suffering, and less toward providing flavored coffee, comfortable chairs, and acres of accessible parking for throngs of upper-middle-class suburbanites. That's not to say wealthy white people don't need God, but c'mon, you know what I mean. This was perhaps the most confusing part of it all, because I really loved my church! I loved the music and the messages and the kids' program, and I loved the people. But the more I learned about Jesus, the more I thought he probably wouldn't have designed the church around . . . well . . . me.

In the beginning, all I knew was that I needed to follow Jesus, and I thought that meant acting like a good Christian. Strangely, the longer I have walked with Jesus, the more strongly I feel that to align myself with the so-called good Christians is to stand in stark contrast against his teaching. When I started down this path, I simply didn't know the difference. I thought a good Christian was a weak man with a strong will, who bent his life around the rule of law, and I imagined Jesus in the same way. But when I really got to know him, what I found in Jesus was a strong man with a *submissive* will, fully and courageously given over to God's wild purpose for the world.

Jesus was just a badass. He was a rule breaker. A system-bucking ball buster. He boldly pushed back against social norms *and* the religious order of the day to engage in his God-given duty to heal the sick, feed the poor, call out injustice, and pave the way for *everyone* to know the saving grace of faith, hope, and love. The world called him weird and the club called him dangerous. They spit on him, they threw things at him, they drove him away, and hell, eventually they killed him. But Jesus was such a motherfucking badass, he just kept loving.

For that kind of life I was not prepared.

When I walked into church for the very first time, I did it *for me*. To fix me. To help me mother my child. To heal my ailing marriage. To redirect my messy life. And to be frank, I didn't really care where the whores and the hobos went to church. I didn't think about enslaved or exploited or starving people. Orphans and widows were not my problem, because I was busy getting myself *right with the Lord*. All I really wanted was to be a good Christian, and then to *sit* and *stay* in that satisfying goodness forever.

My intent to follow Jesus was genuine, but I really wasn't planning on following a fearless leader into battle. I didn't know that this decision might someday draw me into the fight for justice and equality. It never occurred to me that I could be called upon to help tend the wounds of the world, or to push against the order of a broken institution. And I most certainly did not think I was embarking on a journey that would land me in a foreign country or compel me to write a stupid book.

I guess I'm glad I had no idea how much *work* following Jesus would be when I dragged my weary soul into church that first Sunday. I just never imagined that after I learned to sit and stay, I could be asked to stand and go.

7

Years of Plenty

Over the next few years, we added two more little boys to our ranks, becoming a family of five wrapped up in our neatly manicured American dream.

We were the essence of picture-perfect suburbia. I mean, sort of.

We had the house and the hedge and the minivan in the driveway, but I didn't really look old enough to be the mother of three crazy little boys. At the park, strangers assumed I was an exasperated nanny, and at home, solicitors smiled and asked me to get my mom. We also had a three-legged shelter mutt called Peanut, who worked endlessly to set us apart from our dignified neighbors, with their eight-hundred-dollar purebred pups still sporting all four limbs. Despite her disability, Peanut was incredibly fast. She was *constantly* escaping out the front door and running me ragged just trying to catch her. We lived right across the street from the elementary school, and once, during recess, a kid saw this embarrassing spectacle and pointed it out to my boys, shouting, "Look! There's your *babysitter* chasing your *tripod* across the soccer field."

Feeling the need to defend my honor, my oldest puffed up his chest and said, "That lady that looks like a teenager is our *mom!*" And then his baby brother piped up from behind, "And that's not a tripod. It's a *dog!*"

While the shenanigans raged on at home, Steve was out keeping the peace as a deputy sheriff, bringing home the bacon in the form of a government salary, great benefits, and a kick-ass retirement plan. We bought a nice little house in a nice part of a nice town, and our kids did all the things nice suburban kids do, like playing recreational soccer and taking karate lessons and eating pay-by-the-ounce frozen yogurt. We believed we'd chosen the ideal place to raise kids, knowing they would grow up going to National Blue Ribbon public schools, riding their bikes on the sidewalk, and spending the days of their youth gallivanting around on pristine playgrounds with blue foam padding where dirt would normally be.

For all the world, we looked like a successful, happy couple, and in some ways, we really were. But behind closed doors, our relationship continued to be strained by the ongoing demands of parenthood and mutual disappointment. As I got more and more involved with churchy stuff, an almost palpable tension grew between us. Steve became more distant than ever, sometimes going days at a time without speaking to me or looking at me or acknowledging my existence, and I remained

blind to the varying clues that he was seeking fulfill-
ment outside of our marriage in increasingly destructive ways. I wanted to share the incredible things I was
learning about God and about myself. But, wary of
conflict, I avoided the topic of my growing faith almost
as thoroughly as Steve kept his own secrets.

In my baby-Christian zeal, I thought that if only
Steve knew Jesus, everything would get better. So,
week after week, I asked the ladies in my women's Bible
study to pray for my husband, suggesting they ask
God to do things like "soften Steve's heart" and "touch
Steve's spirit."

And I'll be damned if God didn't do exactly that.

While I was still busy cutting a path as a good
Christian, trying to find quiet time in the chaos of my
days between diaper blowouts and kindergarten melt-
downs, openly weeping with my arms raised at Women
of Faith conferences, and reading Francine Rivers novels as if they were academic companion guides to the
Bible, Steve was having his own kind of spiritual awak-
ening.

One day he burst into the house after a particularly
long stretch of contemptuous silence, in which he'd
spent most of his time slamming things around in the
garage or bent over under the hood of his truck. He
stomped in, covered in grease and sweat, and stopped
in the middle of the living room, where I was sitting
on the sofa with one of our little guys in my lap. When
he spoke, I was actually startled by his voice, because

he hadn't said a word to me in about a week, but it was *what* he said that made me feel kind of queasy and light-headed. He gestured down the street in the direction of my neighborhood Bible study, and he hissed, "You can tell all your little friends to stop praying for me."

There was an uncomfortable pause, just enough time to peel my eyebrows off the ceiling, and then with a heavy sigh he added, "I'll go to church with you."

The thing is? I'd never said one word to him about my hope that he would have some kind of come-to-Jesus moment. Granted, having grown up in church, he probably could have hypothesized that his hyper-Christian wife was out there actively lobbying for his eternal salvation. But even Steve will tell you, he *knew* someone was praying for him, because God had gone and softened his heart or touched his spirit or something mysterious like that.

I'd been anticipating this moment for ages, but it wasn't like he was pleased to tell me the news. He sounded furious. The words tumbled out in an angry snarl, and then he stormed away without waiting for a response. Which was good, because I didn't have one. I just sat there unmoving, eyes huge and unblinking, mouth hanging open like, *What the hell just happened?* For a long time I waited for him to come back inside and say he was just messing with me or, better yet, explain exactly how he knew I'd enlisted my entire Christian lady gang to pray for him, but he didn't return.

In the days that followed, neither of us brought up his announcement. The whole thing sort of hovered in the back of my mind like a dream, like maybe it hadn't actually happened. But a stack of pornographic magazines and a can of chew that mysteriously appeared in the outside garbage bin reassured me our brief interaction hadn't just been a figment of my imagination. Whether it was God's divine intervention or Steve's gut reaction I guess we'll never know, but that day *something* prompted him to get his shit together.

I like to think it was God.

———

When I met Jesus as an adult, I slipped into his arms with all the fight of a newborn baby. I needed to be carried. I needed to be nourished. I needed to be protected. And like a newborn in her mother's arms, I completely trusted God to care for me. But Steve met Jesus when he was little. He was introduced to Jesus through Sunday-school scare tactics: shown a picture book of heaven and hell, told that his parents were going to the nice place called heaven, and asked where he wanted to end up. Naturally, because he was like *six*, he wanted to go wherever his mama was going, so he chose to follow her to heaven by inviting Jesus into his itty-bitty heart that very day. So in a way he already knew Jesus was with him, years later, as his life spiraled down into the shadows of his own brokenness. And Jesus hadn't helped.

He'd been hurt and disappointed, so I could completely understand why Steve turned away from church as a young man, and yet I had a hard time understanding why this new prodding from God seemed to make him so angry. But then I'd never been let down by God, the way Steve felt he had. I'd never begged God for freedom from my personal demons only to have them come back at me, time and again, stronger and more overwhelming than ever. I hadn't lived with years of spiritual shame over a perceived lack of faith, or carried around a quiet belief that maybe God was releasing everyone else from the darkness trying to swallow them whole while He let me drown.

I came to the foot of the cross with a tremendous sense of relief, rescued from the scars and insults of a broken world, and I honestly thought that's how it was for everyone. I thought Steve needed only to lay down his burdens—whatever that means. It never occurred to me that, for Steve, Jesus might actually be part of the problem. In order for the two of them to ever be okay, my husband would have to wrestle the image of God out of the distorted picture painted by his early church experience.

All that is to say, *no wonder he was pissed that my friends and I were praying for him.*

When Steve told me he would go to church, it wasn't in anticipation of a happy reunion with the gracious God of his youth. He was merely relenting to the pestering of a Holy Spirit he wasn't glad to hear from. He'd been miserable and depressed for so long, living a life overrun by deceit, guilt, and shame, and when he finally gave in to the idea of going to church, I don't think his plan was to walk in and hand over his junk. He was just trying to get God off his goddamn back.

———

For a time, life was good and God felt near.

We settled happily into the satisfying order of suburbia, letting the rhythm of the school year set the pace for our lives, taking low-key summer vacations, shopping in bulk, and buying our clothes on sale at Old Navy. We weren't wealthy, but we were comfortable, and best of all, with Steve on board, we were becoming a family who was devoted to the service of God in pursuit of faith, hope, and love.

I know that shit sounds corny, but it was blissfully true. We'd taken vastly different paths to get there, but Steve and I had finally landed on the same page in a big way, and it changed everything. Okay, maybe not *everything*. But it changed a lot of things.

The tension in our home gave way to a new dynamic, one of grace and mutual support. We were finally moving in the same direction and we wanted the same things in life. For once, we were actually partners. I had been on this journey for a couple of years when Steve joined me, and it was so exciting to be able to talk with him about Christianity and Jesus and spiritual growth and all the questions that had been growing in the back of my mind. I finally had a safe place to say out loud all the things I'd been thinking, and I was anxious for Steve's input. I'd found a place to belong and, though it was propped up against a ridiculously simplified version of a complicated God, I had a sense of purpose.

For a handful of years, Steve and I had plenty of friends, plenty of rest, and plenty to do, and our lives felt meaningful and good. We took that balance to heart, and to this day we use it as a litmus test for our mental health and spiritual well-being: Are we connected to others? Is our home a place of respite? Does our work matter?

Looking back over that period, I feel a deep longing tinged with bitterness—a longing to return to the grossly self-centered but oh-so-easy faith I once enjoyed, and bitterness because, if not for those years of plenty, I would never have felt such heartbreaking scarcity later on.

8

Bad Christian

In the beginning it was simple. It was easy. It was pleasant and rewarding. It was following the rules and obeying the laws and asking only rhetorical questions. It was just believe in your heart. Just pray. Just forgive. Just show up. It was "because the Bible says." (And the Bible? It was clear.) It was a country club. It was a soul spa. It was a light show. It was come as you are ... *as long you are approved*. And in the beginning, *I was*. I wore the uniform and I spoke the language and I followed all of the rules.

Until I didn't.

Actually, my years in "good Christian" standing were relatively short-lived. It simply wasn't in my nature to conform as heartily and completely to the ways of the church ladies as was required to stay aboveboard in their circles, and I can still clearly recall the first time I got a proper "bad Christian" finger wagging.

It was at one of those meetings for tired moms to

drop their sticky-faced crap factories in child care for two whole hours so we could indulge in adult conversation and sip coffee while it was still hot. I went every week, and when I walked into the room I knew without a doubt I was surrounded by my people—women with spit-up stains on their shoulders and chicken nugget chunks in their hair. Like me, they carried saggy post-baby bellies, dark circles under their eyes, and purses littered with half-eaten granola bars, loose gummy bears, and tattered tampons. Over many months of Tuesday mornings together, we grew into a pretty close group, shouldering one another's burdens while we passed our tightly wrapped newborns around like joints.

We laughed and cried, talked and prayed. We shared good recipes and bad weight-loss advice, and we never lacked for butter or carbs or caffeine, because someone always showed up with a pile of muffins and the coffee flowed freely. It was the land of breast milk and honey, a small break from the daily grind of laundry and diapers and little runny noses.

We had a good thing going, and we were, like, *super* Christian about it.

That moms group was the epitome of all the super churchy things I like to make fun of these days. We read the Left Behind series with earnest concern for the pathetic losers we'd be leaving behind in the dust of our own Rapture. We listened to CDs of harmony-heavy girl bands, collected year after year from massive women's conferences. We baked Amish friendship bread. So yeah, it was like that. But if I'm being totally honest? At the time, that super churchy stuff and those super churchy chicks were super life-giving to me.

Generous and well intentioned, that group of women taught me what it looks like to serve, as I often found myself overwhelmed by the energy of three little boys, and they showed up, again and again, to help in my hour of need. Truly, I probably would not have survived the early years of parenting without the friendship and support of the church ladies, and for that I will always be grateful.

But in the end, it was my experience with their particular brand of faith that tipped the scales of the comfortable Christian life against me.

My public downfall began when the group's ultraconservative alpha leader (every group has one) introduced a new book, which the ladies took on with zeal. It was a heavy-handed how-to guide for women learning to be godly mothers / submissive wives / generous lovers / daughters of the risen king / or whatever. Basically, it was a twenty-two-chapter guilt trip for women with husbands and children.

The author's ideas about a man's strict authority over his wife made me squeamish right off the bat, but no one else was interested in talking about silly things like misogyny or equality or, y'know, domestic abuse. We read that if we disagreed with our husband's opinion, we should serve him his favorite meal and carefully present our concerns as tender thoughts, not personal objections. Sensing I was in the minority in my distaste for this suggestion, I didn't push the issue, but I distinctly thought, *Nope*.

Then we learned it's a woman's responsibility to look pleasing and keep a smokin'-hot body so that her husband won't be tempted to stray. But no worries. If you let yourself go and push your man into an affair, the book tells you how to fix it. First? Hit the gym and get hot again. Then, to heal your marriage after your husband's indiscretion, meet him at the door wearing nothing but a large bow to signify giving yourself to him, like, as a gift of reconciliation. And I said nothing to the group, but in my heart I was like, *Over my chubby dead body*.

There was a chapter about how medication and professional therapy aren't the answer to clinical depression, *because Jesus*, and I almost confessed to the group that I must be a faithless, unrepentant sinner, because I survived every single day with the help of a little blue pill and a licensed counselor. But, again, I didn't speak up. I stayed quiet and kept my thoughts to myself, while in the back of my serotonin-deficient brain, I said, *Bull. Shit.*

With each new week, I signed my kids into child care, poured myself a cup of coffee, and came to the table silently holding a new grudge against that disgusting book. And each week, afraid to raise eyebrows in this group of women I'd come to call friends, I disabled my mouth by filling it with muffins. I bet I gained six pounds before I finally broke my silence.

Of all the things I could have gone donkey nuts over, and there were many, it was "quiet time" that pushed me over the edge.

In this particular chapter, we read about how "quiet time" was crucial to our spiritual lives, which set off a group lamentation about the overall lack of high-quality quiet time. If you're unfamiliar with the concept of quiet time, it's kind of a sacred cow in ladies' church circles. Originating from the ancient discipline of intentionally making space each day to commune with God, today "quiet time" is a spiritual practice most often observed on social media: #quiettime pics usually include a lit candle sitting next to a cup of coffee with visible steam, or maybe a latte with foam art, and an open Bible, preferably out of focus. (It's called "quiet time" because "candle and coffee time" sounds stupid and "prayer time" was apparently already taken.)

Mothers of young children are famous for trying to fit quiet time in during nap time, which also happens to be laundry time, dishes time, shower time, and stare-off-into-space-in-stunned-silence time. From a teething baby to a buzzing dryer to falling asleep at the table with her eyes open, more often than not, quiet time is a total bust for Mama Bear. So it was no surprise when everyone in the group sadly agreed that a daily quiet time seemed like an impossible luxury.

The book, of course, offered a solution for our quiet-time dilemmas. It said, "Get up earlier."

Yup. All you have to do is get up and have your quiet time in the dark before anyone else in the entire world is awake, because "you can sleep when you're dead."

It said that.

For real.

Like, it actually said, "You can sleep when you are dead."

I'm not kidding. A bunch of baby-brained, under-nourished, zombie moms were being told that what they really needed to make their lives better was *less sleep.*

I felt sharply defensive of myself and every other sleep-deprived mother who's put her underwear on backward, sprinkled dry cereal on the floor for her kids, or ordered at a drive-through and mindlessly driven away without her food. Hackles raised, I thought, *I love Jesus, but fuck that shit!* And there were no muffins close enough to stuff in my face, so those exact words came out of my mouth.

The room went record-scratch silent.

I cleared my throat. "I mean . . ."

I swallowed. "Well, what I meant to say is . . ."

I sighed. "Look . . . I just . . . I can't afford to lose any more sleep."

The group leader looked at me with a strange expression, almost bemused by my act of treason. "But surely you're not saying sleep is more important than prayer," she said. "I, for one, am feeling very convicted about the importance of a solid quiet time. God should be our priority."

Then, with the stern determination of a small-town mayor, she declared, "Tomorrow I will be up before sunrise with my candle and my coffee and my Bible. I can sleep when I am dead!"

Heads on either side of her bobbed in agreement, and I knew I should just drop it. But I'm dumb, so I kept going. "Wait a sec," I said. "I love prayer. I'm, like, all about prayer. *Prayer is my favorite!* But I guess I just feel more convicted about being a bad mom because I'm too tired to care for my own kids than I do about not getting up at four a.m. to sit in an empty kitchen reading the Bible by candlelight."

Her reply was meant to sound friendly, but it had the icy edge of righteous indignation. Poking the air with her index finger, she said, "I guess I'd rather be a bad mom than a bad Christian."

And then I dove across the table and punched her right in her smug mouth.

Oh jeez, I'm kidding. *Relax.* I (probably) would never do that.

Actually, I just sat there in silence.

The conversation moved on to the next craptastic chapter (warning parents against the dangers of letting their children get between them—like, *literally*, don't let kids sit or walk or lie in the middle—because only God should be at the center of your relationship; *fix it, Jesus!*), and I sat very still, staring into my coffee. It seemed like the leader was challenging me to make a decision, like I could be a bad mother *or* I could be a bad Christian, and the choice was mine.

How black-and-white.

How very tidy and simple.

How we love to fit our faith into these neat little boxes to be checked off at the end of the day. I thought it must be nice for the people who just know they're doing it right, like they're getting an A in Jesus 101.

Finally I asked, "Why does it have to be quiet?"

I'd been stewing on this for a good ten minutes, and my question was now completely unrelated to the topic at hand.

"Sorry?" The leader turned to me with a hint of irritation.

"Why does quiet time have to be quiet?" There was a distinct note of bitchiness in my voice at this point. "Why can't I spend time with God while I'm running the dishwasher and boiling water and chopping onions for dinner and the TV is blaring to keep my kids occupied?"

The leader blinked hard and tilted her head thoughtfully to one side. She looked at me the way you'd look at a homeless person who's talking to a mailbox. Then she put on her most condescending Sunday-school voice and said, "Because quiet time is a very special time for you to just *be quiet* with God."

I was like, "Yeah. I get that. But if my life is loud, why can't I just *be loud* with God?"

And—I kid you not—she said, "Well, then it wouldn't be *quiet time*, would it?"

For the record, I'm not anti–quiet time. I actually think it's a healthy part of any spiritual life, and I try to make a habit of it now that my kids are pretty much all grown up and out of the way. But this happened when my babies were still babies. And I don't know if you know this, but living with small children is a lot like swimming with piranhas—they may not swoop in and kill you outright, but the nipping and nibbling are relentless.

Sleep was the one thing I knew I had to have if I was gonna be a decent mom for another day. I needed sleep, because my kids needed me to get dressed and go to the park and read the same book four hundred times and kiss boo-boos and settle disputes over Legos and cut a single grape into eleven pieces and scoop turds out of the bathtub and not kill anybody, either by accident or on purpose.

Sleep was life.

I could handle interpretive differences about marriage and womanhood and mental illness that the book stirred up, but nobody was gonna tell me to sleep when I'm dead. That's going too far.

So when the group leader made that little quip about quiet time needing to be quiet, an unexpected volcano of molten outrage burst forth from the depths of my soul. And even though I still stand by what I said next, I do wish I'd said it with a little less . . . *crazy.*

"Oh, for Christ's sake, then call it 'loud time'! Call it 'chaos time.' Call it what it's supposed to be, which is 'intentional time'! But do not tell me that God entrusted three kids to my care and protection—knowing full well what a total energy suck they are—with the expectation that I would keep them all alive and, oh, *also*, get up before the ass crack of dawn to 'be quiet with Him,' because 'I can sleep when I'm dead.'"

I was using finger quotes, like a douche. And I wasn't finished.

In my memory, this impromptu speech is impassioned and articulate, though it's highly unlikely that was actually the case. If only in my head, what I went on to say came out something like this: "I don't think that's how it works. I really don't. I think God is *with us.* Like, day in and day out, in the chaos and the noise and the silliness of life, *He is there.* The God of your precious, untouchable 'quiet time' is a present witness to our nonstop lives, never absent for the clamor of our kids' laughter, their squeals, their skinned knees, their fussing and whining and raging fits in the Target parking lot. God is not withholding Himself from us, waiting for us to come to Him in the wee hours of the morning as a measure of our devotion!

"I mean, if you have the bandwidth to get up an hour earlier every day, with your twelve-dollar scented candle and your fancy French press, good for you! You should totally do that! But don't you dare act like it's some kind of deal breaker for the rest of us. Don't. You. Dare.

"I will *not* be getting up earlier. Nope. I'm gonna honor God intentionally *in my sleep,* because I'm pretty sure God wants me to be the very best mother I can possibly be to my boys. I will listen for God's voice in the wilderness, and at the water park, and under McDonald's indoor play structure, because that is my daily *loud time* and God is faithful to meet me in the chaos. If that makes me a bad Christian, *then I guess I'm a bad Christian.* But tomorrow I'll be sleeping in. And I'm not even gonna worry about it, because I'm pretty sure *I'LL HAVE PLENTY OF QUIET TIME WITH GOD WHEN I'M DEAD!*"

Crickets.

There was no mic drop, no standing ovation, no vigorous applause from my fellow wrung-out baby wranglers. What followed was several long seconds of intensely awkward silence, punctuated by a sniffle on one side of the room and a cleared throat on the other, until someone had the presence of mind to slide the entire tray of muffins to the center of the table. To my great relief, and by the healing touch of simple carbs, life and casual conversation resumed. It was not a rousing victory speech, but still, I did win a battle that day; I expressed a strong difference of opinion in front of the Church Ladies Who Know All Things . . . *and I lived.*

Anyway, the whole point is that long before I became the Very Worst Missionary—hell, long before I became any kind of missionary at all—I had to get comfortable in my own skin as a Pretty Bad Christian.

9

Get Real

In the midst of my growing disillusionment with the club, I soon found myself in the company of a small society of other no-nonsense churchgoers. To the rest of the church community, we were like the kids who smoke under the bleachers, the misfits who suppressed laughter every time the pastor prayed for the Lord to "come in him" or "penetrate him deeply." We had each taken a vastly different route to get there but somehow ended up in the same place—on the outer fringe of Evangelicalism, considered barely more than outsiders by those who occupied the good seats, because of our vocal questions, critical opinions, or (gasp!) progressive theologies.

By then, Steve and I had run the gamut of ministries. We'd done the small groups and the weekend retreats and the golf tournaments and the craft nights. The church had us spread so thin, it was like every day of the week there was somewhere one of us was supposed to be without the other. So, to save our sanity and our family, we swore off all of them and instead looked for a way to serve God and others side by side.

We soon found our ministry niche as leaders in the church youth group, where Steve and I learned that we were happiest when our home was filled with pizza crusts and Cheetos crumbs and packs of wild teenagers. Being in our midtwenties, our relative youthfulness made us a natural fit, but it was Steve's experience as a beat cop and my history as a skanky slut that really gave us an edge. We had good intuition and personal perspective for the complicated lives of the fourteen-to-eighteen crowd.

We welcomed high school kids into our home and into our hearts with genuine love, and without condemnation, and this made us popular with students and parents alike. We became a magnet couple for troubled teens—or, perhaps more precisely, for the fretful parents of troubled teens, who secretly hoped we could transform their kids into good little Christians at a weekend campout, or during a rousing game of "Butts Up."

The youth pastor and his wife quickly became our closest friends, aided by the fact that they weren't just a couple of friends; they were "couple friends." I can't begin to tell you how awesome it is to find couple friends—like, where both of you actually enjoy hanging out with both of them. It's a rare and magical thing to behold, like a nun on a motorcycle, and should be cherished.

Being couple friends allowed us a million hours

together, mostly eating, drinking, and solving all the world's problems. And it was during these many hours that Jeff and Kathy inadvertently demonstrated what it means to "be the church," as they were kind and generous, openhanded with their gifts, and respectful of every individual's faith process. With Jeff and Kathy there were no facades. No masks. No striving to impress.

Jeff was quirky, direct, and abrasive. He didn't waste time with things like polite conversation, and he didn't treat everyone like they deserved his undivided attention. To be honest, he could be kind of a dick if you got in his way—but when you stepped aside, you'd find he was already headed to serve someone specific and you just happened to be standing in his path. Not everyone liked Jeff, and Jeff didn't care, which made me like him even more. I could respect a guy who followed Jesus and was *unapologetically himself.*

And Kathy was my soul sister. She was honest without being arrogant, sweet without being syrupy, loyal without being delusional, and encouraging without being condescending. She was also one of those cool outdoorsy chicks who know how to tie knots and start fires and fight grizzly bears and shit like that. Her house was cute and comfortable enough to make you feel at home, but not so sparkling clean and spectacular that you'd be mortified if you accidentally knocked over your beer during a race for the last piece of pie . . . (cough) . . . or something. She served incredible meals on paper plates and champagne in red Solo cups, and she didn't stress on the rare occasion that dessert might not look as good as it tasted. Through Kathy I learned the value of prioritizing people over perfection.

Eventually, life would take us in vastly different directions (one to the equatorial tropics, the other to the Arctic Circle), but I can say I learned more about how to live like Jesus during the handful of years I had Kathy on my team than from all the other people I know combined.

———

So, there's this funny thing that happens when you get real in front of people: It's that they start to get real in front of you.

Surely you've figured this out by now, but I'll say it anyway: I'm a good faker. Or at least I used to be. I'd played the tough girl, the teen mom, the happy wife, the good Christian, and at twenty-six years old, I still thought I was supposed to look for someone who was better than me, and then be them. Not learn from them or be inspired by them or follow their example—*be them*. I had always believed my own nature was meant to be suppressed and hidden or, if at all possible, *destroyed* to make room for someone better. Someone tougher. Someone smarter. Someone kinder. Someone cooler. Someone else. Always someone else.

But around Jeff and Kathy I could be my own someone. I could be sarcastic and sweary, opinionated, passionate, moody, funny, scared, scarred, and just generally goofy. Not only did they make space for my nature, but they coaxed it out of hiding by show-ing their true colors first. They were just *real*. Around their table we talked freely about our doubts and dis-appointments. We openly shared observations, good and bad, about life and faith and church. We debated. Sometimes we disagreed. But we came in as ourselves and we left as ourselves, and I think this respect for one another's differences elevated our friendship even further.

Jeff was living proof that there could be a place in the church for *the real me*, a darkly brooding, depression-fighting, doubtful, brazen, kinda-bitchy bad Christian. And Kathy's natural bent toward selfless badassery challenged me to serve others in the ways that came the most naturally to me. For the first time in my en-tire life, I felt like I knew who I was. And maybe who I was wasn't so awful and embarrassing and worthless. In fact, maybe who I was was who God had intended me to be all along.

Pretending to be someone else is exhausting. I'd given so much energy to keeping up appearances that when I finally realized I could drop the act altogether, it was like stepping out of a furry suit on a hot summer day. In a word, it was *refreshing*. It was terrifying too, because all of a sudden I was seeing and feeling and ex-periencing the world as my own self, and I felt exposed. But for the first time ever, I also felt *free*.

As a youth group leader, I met with a group of girls every week to talk about everything under the sun. We had sleepovers on my living room floor, watched movies, baked cookies, painted our nails, all while I did my best to answer their hardest questions and address their biggest fears. I learned to say things like "I don't know" and "That's a really good question." But the thing I said most often was "Be who you are."

The one thing I wanted my girls to know deeply, and truly, and forever, was that *who they were* was exactly who God meant for them to be. *Exactly.*

Looking in from the outside, it was easy for me to see how each of them had a place, a spot of their very own to fill, and if they hid who they were by trying to be someone else, the world would miss their one-of-a-kind contribution. Don't get me wrong, we also talked about stuff like character flaws and bad habits and poor choices and personal responsibility. This wasn't about encouraging them to settle into life as their dumb fifteen-year-old selves and never change. I wanted them to mature and grow up, but I wanted them to know and respect who they were in the process. Against the backdrop of a culture hell-bent on convincing them they must become someone better in order to be loved, and in the shadow of a church telling them they needed love in order to become someone better, I told the girls in my group, honestly and often, that I loved them most when they were most themselves.

What Jeff and Kathy did for Steve and me we tried

to do for the students who passed through our lives each week. We shared our truest selves and made space for the kids in our groups to do the same. For some, our home became a haven, a welcome place where vulnerability would be honored and where honest questions would get honest answers. In us we hoped they would find no false pretenses, no pretending, and no one to impress, so they'd never feel the need to be anyone but themselves.

Hannah was a student in my small group for a few years. She was a pastor's kid who played the drums and the guitar and sang in the worship band. According to our kids, she was the best babysitter ever, and one summer she even taught my younger boys how to swim. Once, when she was being kind of a dipshit, she challenged me to a friendly fight, so I wrestled her to the ground, sat on her back, and rode her like a donkey, just to show her who was boss. Hannah was so much fun, but she was also a deep thinker with a tender heart and a sort of tortured soul. The day she told me she needed to talk, I had a pretty solid idea what it was gonna be about.

Hannah laughs when she gets nervous, and also, she cries. I knew the instant she walked through the door that her nerves were firing on all cylinders, because she was a chuckling, teary-eyed mess.

Steve was at work and the boys were in bed, so it

was just the two of us in an unusually quiet house. She sat down at the kitchen table, and I immediately set a giant plate of oatmeal-raisin cookies in front of her. They were her favorite, and I thought it would be helpful to pile at least two dozen on a plate and shove them right in her face. For a while she was quiet, sort of picking at a cookie, pressing loose crumbs together with her fingertip, until she looked up at me with a tightly knit brow and her dark eyes welling with tears.

I know that face, I thought. *That's the face of a faker.*

Finally, with a deep breath, Hannah took off the mask she'd worn for her whole life and told me she was gay.

She'd been working so hard for so long to deny her own nature, to be someone else, someone worthy, someone good, someone lovable, and she was simply exhausted. She decided to say it out loud, because she couldn't carry the weight alone any longer.

I will never know the kind of courage Hannah showed that day.

I will never have the kind of balls it must have taken for her to knock on my stupid suburban door, and sit at my lame IKEA table, and cut herself wide open for me to really see the girl who was drowning beneath a pile of labels she didn't choose—"pastor's kid," "tomboy," "straight girl." Hannah was already doing at sixteen what I was still learning at twenty-six; she was claiming her own self, taking ownership of all of who she was. And even though she was afraid because she didn't know how or where she was going to fit into the world or the church, or even her own family, she would at least be free to find out.

Our church, the church where Hannah's dad was a larger-than-life pastor who looked like a Ken doll and talked like a radio DJ, wasn't "gay affirming." Remember, this was way back in the day, before inclusive churches and affirming Christians were even part of the bigger conversation. To be perfectly honest, I hadn't given it much thought prior to that night, and the only thing I'd heard from the church on the subject was "It's a sin. Duh." I'd heard some debate about nature versus nurture. I'd read some stuff about the horror of "conversion camps." I'd seen the news coverage of the scandalized hellfire preacher who'd been caught getting blow jobs from dudes in public restrooms. I'd driven past those disgusting picketers with signs declaring, "God Hates Fags." So I knew it was a cruel world in which to be a gay teenager, but, I'm embarrassed to admit, until then it had all seemed too distant for me to take an interest. But now here was Hannah in my kitchen, and Hannah was *mine*. She had a place in my heart, in my family, in my community, and I realized that in that moment my opinion or lack thereof didn't matter at all. My only job in the universe was to hold her up, to share her burden, to help her become her own someone.

I'm sure I said a few well-meaning things I wish I could take back today, but I don't remember. I remember admitting that I didn't really know what I thought about being gay, and I tried to remind her that the Bible has been translated for us and taught to us mostly by straight white dudes, and I wasn't sure if I fully trusted those interpretations.

At the time, I didn't know if I thought gayness was a sin or not. I didn't know what her parents would say. I didn't know what her future held. And I didn't know what she should do next.

But I did know some things. God loved her and I loved her, I knew that much for sure, and I believed we both loved her best when she was wholly herself, because I knew without a doubt that who she was was exactly who God had made her to be.

Exactly.

Last year Hannah got married, and I had the immense privilege of walking her down the aisle on her wedding day. What an honor it was to be by her side, once again, as she took a huge step forward in life. Knowing the difficult path she has walked so bravely, seeing Hannah calmly delivered into the arms of her beautiful bride, will always be one of the proudest moments of my life.

During the ceremony, I had an opportunity to say a prayer over their marriage, and then I lifted my arms to hug them both at once. When I did this, the knee-length dress I'd chosen for the occasion pulled up far enough to expose my dimply white thighs where they gooshed out from a pair of flesh-colored Spanx, like two enormous links of chicken sausage. This happened in front of at least 150 people with cameras aimed and ready, and I probably should have been mortified, but honestly? I didn't even care.

I'm no longer a stranger to being exposed, and if there is anything I truly know and understand about this world, it's that this amazing thing happens when people see the realest parts of the real you: They trust you with their realness too.

10

Adventure Us

The first time I boarded a plane bound for Costa Rica, I couldn't have told you where to find it on a world map. Was it an island? Was it in South America? Was it populated by angry tribal warriors with loincloths and poison darts? No idea. When other people found out I was going there on a mission trip, they asked me these questions like I should have answers, and I just looked at them like, *What am I,* National Geographic?

I was headed to this mysterious land as an adult leader with our youth group for my first experience as a short-term missionary, which also happened to be my first trip abroad. We emerged from our plane into the heavy air of the tropics mixed with the smog of a busy city and the smells of wet earth and motor oil. Welcome to Costa Rica. Along with Steve and a dozen excited teenagers, I made my way through customs and immigration at Juan Santamaría International Airport. Despite the fact that I carried no illegal contraband of any kind, I was sweating like a drug mule, convinced that at any moment I would be arrested, strip-searched, and left to rot in a slimy jail cell.

I was so busy dreaming up worst-case scenarios, it didn't even cross my mind to imagine the best— that the first stamp in my passport could be the first of many. In the years to follow, that stiff new passport would become soft and worn, permanently bent from being jammed in the back pocket of my jeans, ink smudged by moist palms, and dog-eared from being tossed into bags and backpacks and hastily retrieved a thousand times. But that day, as I inched through the line to enter another country for the first time, with armpit stains the size of dinner plates, it was inconceivable to me that someday the pristine passport I so gingerly handed to a bored Costa Rican immigration agent would be filled with stamps from cover to cover, country to country, including pages I'd have to have added.

But before any of that could happen, we would have to make the unimaginable leap from volunteering a few days a week as youth group leaders and chaperoning the occasional short-term trip to living overseas as international missionaries. So what happened, you may wonder, to make a cop and a soccer mom decide to sell all their shit, pack their bags, and drag their kids on a grand adventure? I mean, seriously. What were we thinking?

To tell you the truth, we had no good reason to shake things up. We could have kept on living our safe, comfortable lives in the suburban sprawl of California's Gold Country indefinitely. Sometimes I wish we had. We could have endured the sparkly light show at church every weekend and been present to invest in the lives of the students we loved. We could have enjoyed watching our sons grow up surrounded by grandparents, aunts, and uncles. We could have simply remained there, basking in the steady glow of a God who, at the time, felt especially present.

Before that first trip to Costa Rica, our lives were pleasant, fulfilling, and so damn easy. And sometimes I wish we'd stayed right there, in that beige house with the three-legged dog, in that city, with those people, collecting that sweet-ass paycheck and hosting groups of rowdy teenagers for as long as they would let us.

But we didn't.

You know why?

Because we're idiots.

Also because, together, Steve and I were beginning to believe that God was calling us out into the world to do something bigger, something *better.* We'd started to suspect that we were supposed to be part of something *awesome.*

But mostly it's because we're idiots.

———

It might be important to note that before we became missionaries, we accidentally became the kind of people who could become accidental missionaries.

Just before our first brief foray into Christian missions by way of Costa Rica, Steve and I discovered we had a taste for travel when we packed our kids and an ice chest into our minivan and hit the open road for a cross-country trip, guided by nothing more than the path that lay ahead and our heart's desire. This was our first real family adventure and, like many to follow, it was stupidly impulsive, poorly planned, underestimated, over budget, and super memorable.

We drove nearly eight thousand miles, from California to Florida, up the East Coast, and back through the Midwest, hitting twenty-three states and stopping along the way to see friends and family, view national treasures, and visit roadside oddities. Bear in mind, this was before GPS and cell phones and screen time. My husband and I were the only navigation, education, and entertainment systems on board, so the success of the trip was completely dependent upon our ability to read a paper map, recall fifth-grade U.S. history, and keep three kids spanning six years of age from crying out of sheer boredom.

When our plan to "hit the road and see what happens" went well, it went very well. Like the night we pulled into a parking lot at the Grand Canyon around midnight. We slept there for a few hours and then sneaked out onto the trail before dawn to watch the morning mist burn off with the rising of the sun. We led our boys through the dark to a flat spot on a rock outcrop, where we sat and snuggled together wrapped in blankets to watch the show, as if God Himself were pulling back the curtain to reveal His spectacular creation. Turns out, sunrise at the Grand Canyon is no joke.

Another day we pulled off the interstate for gas and realized we were only a few blocks away from the French Market in New Orleans. Of course we detoured to do a little shopping and went on to explore the rest of the city. Happy to be out of the car for a while, we walked through the Garden District, utterly charmed by the stunning architecture and giant old oak trees dripping with moss. The day grew more and more humid as we strolled, and we were pretty relieved when we turned a corner into a big park with a path that looked like it would take us straight back to our car. It started off like a typical bike path, but we soon found ourselves stepping over bundles of cords, around large toolboxes, and between folding chairs, until someone official-looking approached us with his hands held out, fingers splayed, in the universal sign for *Oh my god, you're ruining everything*, and hissed, "Please be quiet, we're shooting a scene!"

We were so busy being dumb tourists, we'd accidentally walked right into the middle of a film set. By that time, our kids were tired and hungry, and, it should be noted, it was a *hot* August day in New Orleans and we are California-dry-heat kind of people. Our hair had melted down onto our purple-red faces, and our clothes were wet, see-through, and stuck against our bodies with unholy levels of perspiration. Let's just say we didn't look normal or . . . *healthy* . . . which is probably why they let us keep walking through the set to take the quickest route back to our car.

That's how we ran into a young Scarlett Johansson as she was being primped and powdered by busy hands in preparation for her next scene. We didn't know who she was at the time, only that, whoever she was, she was, like, Hollywood important, and she wasn't happy to see us. She looked physically frightened by our family, Steve in particular, as though she thought he was planning to reach out and slash her face or something. I thought, *Sheesh. What a prissy bitch.* But in retrospect, we did look like actual swamp monsters, so I guess it's not her fault for mean-mugging us like we were freaks.

Eventually we managed to extricate ourselves from the live set of *A Love Song for Bobby Long* (which also starred John Travolta and went straight to video in 2004), and we trudged on. About half a block from our car, we met a guy who could tell by our sweatiness that we weren't from the South. This man was tan and blond with crystal-blue eyes, and his shirt was not stuck to his body. He was one of those true southern gentlemen: forward, genial, super polite. He struck up a conversation, and we paused to chat for a minute, and when he invited our disgusting family into his beautiful historic home for a "cold lemonade" in that smooth New Orleans drawl, I practically swooned. Unfortunately, we had to decline his kind invitation because he was probably a serial killer. *But still.*

More often than not, the no-plan plan worked in our favor, and we enjoyed daily surprises along our route, although from time to time things didn't pan out exactly how we would have liked.

Without the benefit of TripAdvisor, we were flying blind, usually pulling up to the first cheap motel with a neon vacancy sign and a free breakfast. If I were to write reviews of the rooms we slept in over the span of the trip, I'd say they mostly ranged from "Could use a good cleaning" to "Pretty sure someone died in here." On the worst night, we ended up in the middle of nowhere at 10:00 p.m., forced to quit driving by exhaustion and an accumulation of delayed potty breaks. We stopped at the only place we'd seen in ages, which happened to be a Motel 6 flanked by two strip clubs. This alone would have been fine, except that all the other rooms were occupied by a minor-league baseball team. We had to keep the TV on all night with the volume turned way up to protect our children's innocence.

Back home, tales from this trip earned us a reputation for being *adventurous* and *spontaneous.* Like the one where we accidentally followed a one-lane road that ended at a river ferry preparing for its next departure and, rather than turn back, we drove right onto the ferry and landed in historic Jamestown, Virginia. Or when we visited a "museum" somewhere in the middle of Kansas that was really just a hoarder's house at the end of a dirt road surrounded by cornfields. It was filled with odds and ends like creepy dolls, two-headed animal taxidermy, and fetal pigs floating in jars of formaldehyde. We paid something like two dollars apiece to enter and wander through a little old man's junk piles, and it was weird, but I felt kind of proud of him for at least turning a small profit on his dysfunction.

It was a great trip, a wild and wonderful family vacation. And it plays a pivotal role in the story of how we decided to sell off our easy suburban life and move to a foreign country.

See, it takes a certain amount of confidence and—let's be real—a hefty dose of arrogance to believe that God is calling you to go out into the world and "be the hands and feet of Jesus," especially when you don't speak the language, don't understand the culture, and can't find the freakin' place on a map. I'm not saying perfectly humble missionaries don't exist, just that the recipient of such a call must be more than a little self-assured of their ability to handle the challenges that come with such a move. On some level, they have to believe that they are intrepid enough to overcome any challenge and flexible enough to deal with any circumstance of living in a foreign environment. In other words, they need to be *adventurous* and *spontaneous*.

You see where I'm going with this?

Yeah.

Steve and I went on our first short-term mission trip less than a year after we went on a crazy cross-country escapade where we discovered that *we* were adventurous and spontaneous. Whenever anyone from our church found out we would be chaperoning the youth-group kids on a trip to Costa Rica, they said things like "You two are so *adventurous*, I could see you packing up and moving there!" or "You two are so *spontaneous*, I wouldn't be surprised if you never came back!"

Thus the seed was planted.

Our wildly spontaneous family adventure preceded our first trip to Costa Rica as youth-group leaders by a matter of months. We made two more trips with teenagers in subsequent years, and aside from a few minor snags here and there (a kid stepped on a nail, the van got a flat tire, I had to yell at some students over a five-dollar dare to take a dump in the volcanic hot springs, etc.), each trip went off without much drama. The North American kids were paired off with Costa Rican kids to stay in homes for a true "Tico" experience, and each evening everyone came together for a barbecue or a soccer game or just to hang out.

It hadn't yet occurred to me to wonder about the real value or long-term purpose of these trips, but even in retrospect, as far as short-term mission trips go, I think this was actually a pretty decent experience for everyone involved.

We were there in partnership with a local youth

group for the mutual exchange of ideas and cross-cultural exposure (which included bringing the Tico youth group to the United States for their own short-term mission trip). While we were there, it was somewhat challenging for the North American kids, but there was no opportunity for gross self-congratulation, no pretending to change the world. They might not have had hot water or a washing machine at their disposal, but in Costa Rica, our high school students went to the mall and the movies, they played video games, they passed car dealerships, they ate at Papa Murphy's pizza and Burger King. They saw the many ways in which Costa Rican teenagers are their smart, funny, capable peers and not their poor, needy, incompetent counterparts.

Since I didn't grow up going to church, the missionaries who hosted us were the first missionaries I'd ever met. (Here's an embarrassing confession: For a really long time—I mean, like, *way too long*—I thought *missionaries* were *mercenaries*. So I would pray, like, "Lord God, watch over your missionaries. Bless all those bad-ass motherfuckers who sneak into heavily guarded compounds under cover of night with hand grenades and rocket launchers to rescue foreign dignitaries and high-ranking hostages from the clutches of evil." But then, I also thought it was "for all *intensive* purposes" well into my thirties, so now you know exactly what kind of person you're dealing with.)

The missionaries we spent time with seemed pretty

cool and down-to-earth, but mostly they just seemed like regular people. A few of them might even be the kind Steve and I would be friends with if we lived right down the street; they liked beer with lime and salt, meat cooked over fire, and off-color jokes. We said things to each other like "We could actually hang out with these guys."

And so it was on our last flight home from a short-term trip to Costa Rica that Steve leaned close to me and said, "I'm going to say something crazy, but I don't want you to freak out."

I said, "Oookaaay?" and acted like he was being dumb even though I knew exactly what he was going to say, because I was just about to say the same thing.

He whispered, "I think we should become missionaries."

And I nodded. "Me too."

He said, "I really think we could do it."

And I agreed, "Me too."

And then we both looked a little bit ill, like maybe we'd just invoked the Holy Spirit to set our house on fire. Which, in a way, we had. We just didn't know it yet.

Here's what we *did* know:

1. Based on the grand total of twenty-seven days we'd spent there, we thought Costa Rica would be a super cool place to live.
2. Normal people could be missionaries.

3. We were normal people! . . . Okay, normal*ish*.
4. We were on the same page, like, actually in agreement over this pretty major life-changing thing, when we usually couldn't even agree on where to eat.
5. We were *adventurous* and *spontaneous*.
6. Please. What more could Jesus want?

PART 3

What in the Actual Hell

11
Raise Your Hand

Since I've done it, people always ask me how to become a missionary. I'm happy to share, but sometimes it's hard to tell if they feel relieved or appalled by my answer, because I usually just shrug and say, "All you have to do is raise your hand."

Sure, there are a few other details that need to be managed. You have to find a church or church organization to sponsor you, raise funds, buy Crocs—but the only real requirement for you to go *anywhere you want*, to do *anything you want*, and to have other people pay for it is that you have to *volunteer*.

Oh, and don't forget to say it's for Jesus, because, let's be honest, if you say God is "calling you," who's gonna argue?

If you don't already have a specific plan or goal for your mission, no worries. Every day a soulful hipster from a sceneless small town in Nebraska decides he needs to *go* and *be present* as a coffee-shop missionary in Portland, or a young Spanish major from Atlanta makes a case for the necessity of her very Christ-like *presence* for a summer in Madrid. But Steve and I didn't really like that idea of being present. We were new to the missions game, but even we could see that it's kind of stupid to pay someone to drink coffee and read novels and be friendly to random strangers in some destination-quality city like it's their job.

No, seriously, we wanted our work to have purpose, and not just the made-up kind. We wanted to do something worthwhile, and while we did that special something, our plan was to "love on people" (*yeesh*), get involved in the community, and make organic connections with our neighbors. (Let's not talk about how we were already doing this quite effectively where we lived. It bums me out too much.)

The world was at our fingertips, and with nothing to hold us back, we struggled to figure out where God wanted us to go and what He wanted us to do. So we turned to the professionals. We applied to the missionary-sending agency we'd become familiar with through our trips to Costa Rica, and we thought it made sense to ask them for help with our dilemma. Since we were so adventurous and spontaneous, we told them we were open to going to work *anywhere*, and we figured these people who sent batches of missionaries out three or four times every year would help us narrow down our choices.

We didn't want to go for the sake of going, and we didn't want to go wherever we felt like going. We wanted to go where God could use us, where the mission needed us, and where the people would want us. Steve and I spent months talking about it, praying over it, and seeking the right place for our family. He'd always been a handy guy, and he dreamed of leading building projects and working side by side with other guys. I still loved my work with high school and college girls, and hoped for a way to carry that over somehow.

It's kind of hard to explain how we ended up deciding on Costa Rica as the right place for us to go. All I can say is this: It felt like we'd been asking God to tell us where to go for a long time, so when an American missionary on the Costa Rican leadership team served us our dream jobs on a silver platter, the invitation to live and work in Costa Rica was too good to pass up. Steve was offered a job managing work teams and overseeing the physical operations of the mission's buildings and facilities, and I was enticed by an "awesome opportunity" to work with a "great program" for college interns (which, it turned out, didn't actually exist).

Looking back, I have a hard time thinking about that conversation without feeling like we were blatantly lied to. I mean, maybe it wasn't an *outright lie*, more like a car salesman's lie—the leaving out of certain facts and information to make the situation appear more appealing than it really was. And maybe it wasn't even as sinister as that. It's possible we were sold on an idea that came from the glowing perspective of a dreamy (albeit entitled) optimist, one who viewed the world through missionary-colored lenses.

After we received an official invitation to join the team in Costa Rica, we went to bed starry-eyed, and the very next morning we set about preparing for an international move. We had to break the news to our families. We had to get rid of all our crap. We had to rent out our house. Or sell our house. Or rent it? Or sell it? We had to *decide* what to do with our house. We had to host a silent auction, followed by thirty-five garage sales and twelve trips to Goodwill. But most of all, we had to figure out how to ask everyone we'd ever met for money. (We were going out as "support-based" missionaries, which means your paycheck comes from a combination of corporate church giving, fifty bucks a month from random old ladies, and a fat check from your husband's parents.)

It took six months for us to sell off our junk, rent out our house, and raise the funds required by the sending agency. Or I should say, it *only* took us six months, because for real? Look around your house and imagine selling or dispersing every bit of it, piece by piece. Furniture, dishes, mattresses, art, books, board games, wooden spoons, mixing bowls, picture frames, toys, tools, everything in every basket, drawer, and cupboard, and don't forget the garage / attic / yard / shed / junk drawer, nearly all of your clothes and shoes, your waste baskets, your potted plants—everything must go! It was a big job and it went surprisingly fast, and while it wasn't easy, it didn't feel like it was as hard as it should have been.

We turned our lives upside down like an old sofa,

shaking out every loose penny, stale cracker, lost re-
mote, and dried-up marker until there was nothing
left to do but drag it out to an empty field and set it
on fire. We *destroyed* the life we knew. By the time we
were done, we were out of a job and out of a home, and
we could carry everything we owned in ten duffel bags
and five backpacks, but finally we were ready to go in
every way!

Except for all the ways we weren't.

There were a few little things that had me worried, like how we didn't speak Spanish, and how our
kids had never even seen their future country of resi-
dence, and how, just weeks before our departure, Steve
and I got in a massive fight, and when he threatened
to call the whole thing off, I threw the phone at him
and yelled, *"Do it!"* He dialed the agency's number on
speaker, and when it started to ring, we both lost our
resolve and agreed to hang up. We each knew the other
was bluffing, because we both knew we were in way too
deep to turn around.

I'm sure it's natural to be filled with fear and anxiety when you're dragging your family to a foreign
country where none of you speak the language and
you're only loosely acquainted with a handful of people
you've barely met. Anyone would have second-guessed
themselves in our situation. We were still excited to
get to Costa Rica, and we still believed we were following God, but the closer it got to go time, the more we
started to see some of the holes in our process. Once it
was just us and the duffel bags, we could see ourselves

more clearly, because all of a sudden there was nothing left to hide behind. Our marriage now looked terribly precarious, our confident kids seemed sad and confused, and our personal demons were clearly alive and kicking.

But we'd volunteered for this, and we had every intention of moving forward. Besides, even if we had wanted to back out, it's hard to argue with the Christian narrative that promises your only job is to raise your hand and show up, and then God will sprinkle pixie dust all over your life. And it's still kind of embarrassing to admit this, but in the deep, dark recesses of my heart, I was holding on to a secret hope that if we obeyed God—like, if we made this great big dramatic sacrifice and became missionaries—*God would fix us.* We would serve God, and God would heal our hurts.

It seemed like a fair trade.

Before we left for Costa Rica, we drove to Chicago to attend a five-week missionary training thingy. It was very serious. There was homework to do and papers to write, team-building classes, guest speakers, and even a course in language acquisition. To experience diversity we went on field trips to cultural centers: a Muslim mosque, a Hindu temple, a Mexican restaurant. Cross-cultural instruction also included playing games where half the people in the room wore a green plastic hat and a sock on one hand, and then the rest of us had to figure out what the deal was with the hats and the socks by overcoming a fake language barrier. Interesting concept, though awkward in practice, but it was all in good fun. When they taught about fund-raising, they mentioned starting a blog to keep our family and friends up to date on our work, and they said that would keep the cash rolling in. Steve took diligent notes and did most of the homework, and I did my part by listening to "Recycled Air" by the Postal Service on repeat and crying myself to sleep.

And *that*, my friend, is how, after six months of begging for money and five weeks of missionary "training," Steve and I landed in Costa Rica with nothing more than our shiny blue passports and three travel-weary children. Ten duffel bags followed us off the plane, and what was in them at that point was anybody's guess.

We tried so hard to be smart with our limited luggage space, but it was unbelievably difficult to decide what was important enough to take and what wasn't. There is no premade packing list for "moving indefinitely to the tropics with three boys of varying ages." I swear, ten minutes before we left for the airport, we were *still* trying to figure it out—packing, unpacking, repacking—frantically trying to weed out all but the most important items. It was pure insanity. Finally, with five seconds left on the clock, we grabbed everything left within arm's reach, shoved it wherever it would fit, and ran out the door. Great plan! Highly recommend this method. Things that made it to Costa Rica included a men's XL cold-water wetsuit, *with flippers*; a gallon-sized ziplock bag full of broken crayons and chewed-up, eraserless pencils; an out-of-date hard-bound *Guinness Book of World Records*; several pairs of mittens; and a shoe without a mate. We'd spent months preparing for that moment, and somehow we still managed to bring about 150 pounds of useless crap with us.

Sadly, I can't recall much about the first day of our first year in Costa Rica. Only that as we slowly made our way through customs and immigration, my charming boys got into a heated argument over who had to poop the most, who had pooped last, and who would poop biggest as soon as they got a chance to poop. Judging by the lingering cloud of farts that followed us through the line, I'm guessing it was a three-way tie.

We arrived at night, and a couple of our new teammates were waiting outside in the heavy Costa Rican air to pick us up in two cars. Steve went with the luggage in one car, and I took the kids in the other. They immediately fell asleep in the backseat of the big white SUV that would take us through the city of Heredia and winding up the mountain in the dark. The driver and I made small talk (he and his wife would become some of our dearest friends), but it was all I could do to keep it together while I watched the colorful little houses and barred storefronts streak by in the headlights. I didn't know a person could feel so happy and so sad at the same time.

I had raised my hand.

I showed up.

Now it was God's turn to do something.

12

Surprise

Our first year in Costa Rica was full of surprises. We were surprised to learn what we loved (mango) and what we hated (papaya), and sometimes we were surprised by what surprised us. Like a coffee field in full bloom across a rolling hillside, an unexpected sea of fragrant white flowers waving in the breeze. There were good surprises, like the full flavor of a ripe banana plucked right off the tree. *Surprise! That's what a banana is supposed to taste like!* And there were some not-so-good surprises, like parasites. *Surprise! You just shit your pants.*

Each new day of our first year in Costa Rica seemed like its own adventure. We woke up on bright, sunny mornings to the bitter, burned-toast smell of coffee roasting in the valley and fell asleep at night to the sound of geckos chirping. Our weekends were filled with expeditions to white-sand beaches, misty green rain forests, and lively farmers' markets, and I was struck with awe and wonder by the simple fact that we were there. I experienced a new kind of fullness as I fell in love with the remarkable little country we were lucky enough to call home. It was so unbelievable to me that we lived there, I felt compelled to announce at least six times a day, *"We actually live here!"*

Y'know, just in case anyone forgot.

I loved the lush tropical paradise that Costa Rica is known for, but I was surprised by how much I also loved the chaos and grit of Costa Rica's city streets. You can be overwhelmed from all sides by the constant beeping of car horns and the blaring of music—rhythmic reggaeton, brassy salsa, and cumbia's wicked accordion riffs—all pouring simultaneously from open windows. Even the rumble of diesel engines and the chugging of buses at stoplights manage to add something more than choking fumes to the atmosphere. When you're in the mood, the activity of San José is just kind of delicious.

The sidewalks were crowded with people walking, people standing together under eaves, people tucked back into recessed doorways to chat. On the street, age and economic status flowed together, from slick young men in crisp suits and pointy polished shoes to leathery old women with aprons tied over faded housecoats. In the afternoon, young kids in school uniforms walked hand in hand with their curvy Latina moms, who teetered along in stilettos and skintight jeans, turning heads and collecting catcalls with swinging hips and sloshing cleavage. From dawn till dusk, the flurry, smog, and din never let up, and when you threw in an abundance of tourists and stray dogs, it made for prime people watching.

In all fairness, the bad surprises usually resulted from our inexperience or silly assumptions about the climate and/or the culture.

For example, if you grew up in California's dry Central Valley, you don't think about what happens to clothes jammed in the back of your closet during thirty-seven consecutive days of rain at one million percent humidity. Move to Costa Rica and pull out a T-shirt you haven't worn in a while? *Surprise! There are mushrooms growing in the creases.*

Or, for example, if you've had a longtime love affair with all things baked and carby, you've probably developed certain expectations for the cakes, doughnuts, and breads in your life. So when you move to Costa Rica, the abundance of bakeries showcasing beautiful pastries in their windows makes your heart go pitter-patter. But when you take your first bite? *Surprise! It's a trick!* It smells delicious, but that golden baguette is so hard and dry you could use it to bludgeon an intruder.

I was also surprised by allergies. I'd never had allergies before, but as rainy season kicked into high gear, I learned that I'm quite allergic to the mold that thrives in Costa Rica's damp conditions. Our youngest son fell victim as well, and the two of us coughed, hacked, and sneezed almost constantly, watching the clock impatiently, like junkies, waiting for the next dose of antihistamines that would give us relief.

Oh, and one other thing I hadn't expected? I ended up being really bad at Spanish. I mean, *really bad*. Like, I talk Spanish even more worser than I does English.

———

Steve and I were supposed to spend our first year abroad learning Spanish together at a language school for missionaries, but after only one semester, our team leaders asked if Steve could ditch school and start work, and (no surprise) he said yes. He was stoked about this change of plans, because *school is lame*, and I was happy for him, but I was also super jealous.

For the rest of the year, I studied Spanish in a tiny classroom with sweaty missionaries while he commuted an hour across the valley to work and learn Spanish by immersion in the community. He picked up the language quickly in the company of his new Costa Rican friends and coworkers, and in no time he was spouting slang and swearing a blue streak like a true Tico. Which, of course, made me even more jealous.

During the first trimester of classes I'd done pretty well, which was unfortunately misinterpreted by the school's administration as aptitude. They moved me into a more advanced group the following trimester, and from day one I was behind. I had missed some of the fundamental building blocks of the language, which left me dazed and confused and revealed the fact that I *did not* have an aptitude for Spanish.

I began to think I would never complete a sentence in Spanish that actually made sense. *Never.* And, it turns out, learning a second language is extra hard for a perfectionist head case, because making mistakes is an unavoidable part of the process. I tried to relax and practice my new grammar and vocabulary on the unlucky locals who crossed my path, but this usually led to looks of confusion or amusement, and sometimes pity. Once, when I really felt like I was getting the hang of things, a friendly grocery-store clerk handed me my receipt and said, in Spanish, "Thanks for shopping at Mas X Menos. Come back soon." Feeling confident, I smiled and tried to sound casual as I replied, *"¡Sí! Volveré pronto porque tengo que comer mi familia!"* which sounds lovely but translates to "Yes! I'll be back soon, because *I have to eat my family.*"

I said that. Somebody shoot me, please.

As I realized my mistake, a permanent anxiety about speaking Spanish became my new normal. Remember after 9/11 when Homeland Security used color-coded "terrorist threat level" advisories to warn the American public? This was a lot like that, but instead of feeling threatened by foreign terrorists, I felt humiliated by my own foreignness in general. I was walking around at Awkward Encounter Level Orange, and with each new embarrassment ("My son has seven anuses"), I became more afraid to open my stupid mouth.

I know you probably already thought of this, but when you live in a Spanish-speaking country, *not* wanting to speak Spanish is (*surprise*) kind of a big deal.

It's not like I thought it would be easy. Learning Spanish was on our list of Very Hard Things we were ready to deal with in our first year in Costa Rica. We had planned on the move being difficult. We'd talked about it often, trying to prepare our kids for the road ahead, and it was hard in all the ways we'd anticipated. But speaking Spanish didn't feel challenging to me anymore; it felt *impossible*. Steve was working so much, he usually wasn't around to help with dinner and the kids' homework and showers and bedtime. Sometimes he'd be gone for a solid week to manage the work teams that came in from the United States or the UK. He took to his new role with all the joy and vigor of a hipster at a mustache convention, but when he was gone, I was left alone to do humiliating things like call a taxi or order a pizza in my hillbilly Spanish.

As I fell further behind in my classes, the barking cough I attributed to allergies stopped responding to over-the-counter medication. When simply taking a breath became a laborious act, one of my classmates (who'd been a nurse in the States) insisted that I see a doctor. The thought of surviving a doctor's appointment with my limited capacity to communicate made me want to run into traffic. Fortunately, a North American doctor saw patients out of a little office right there at the language school one day a week, so all I had to do was write my name in any open time slot on the clipboard hanging from his door—no Spanish required. *¡Gracias a Dios!*

The doctor was a short, serious man, and very ... uh ... *thorough*. After he listened to my heart and lungs, he handed me a tissue and asked me to blow and, assuming he was going to look up my nose, I did as instructed. Instead he took the wad of used tissue, unwadded it, and proceeded to gaze into my warm snot with the intensity of a boardwalk fortune-teller. After a long search, he tossed the tissue in the garbage and declared with the authority of a class A snot inspector, "You have an infection."

He wrote me a prescription for a strong antibiotic, which I took directly to the pharmacy across the street, silently sliding it across the counter to the pharmacist, who immediately produced the prescribed medication in a glass vial with a needle and a syringe. Because (*surprise*) in Costa Rica antibiotics are often given as injectables—*and sometimes you do it yourself!*

I later learned the pharmacist would have given me the shot if I'd asked—he probably even offered—but at that point my Spanish brain was not prepared for medical/pharmaceutical terms. I was still working on stuff like "*Por favor, señor,* how much for one potato?" I certainly wasn't prepared to respond to a stranger who says, "If you'd like to step behind this curtain and drop your pants, I'll inject that in your butt cheek for you."

I went back to school and set the little bottle and the syringe on the desk in front of my nurse friend, and she didn't hesitate for a second. It was a butt-sized needle, but using a deft hand, she was kind enough to deliver the goods through my upper arm. Sadly, a few days later, I returned to the doctor showing no signs of improvement. Everything hurt. My lungs were on fire, and each breath sent shooting pains through my back and chest. For a long time he listened to me breathe, moving his stethoscope here and there, until, putting a kind hand on my shoulder, he said gently, "I think you have pneumonia, and I'd like to admit you to the hospital."

Surprise! You can get pneumonia in paradise.

Maybe it was anxiety mixed with exhaustion, or maybe it was the lack of oxygen to my brain, but at the mere suggestion of hospitalization, I kind of lost my mind. I plainly told him no, and then I gave him all the reasons I couldn't and wouldn't be going to the hospital that day. My husband was gone. My kids needed me at home. I had to study. I had a Spanish test. I had laundry on the line. I had to put a chicken in the Crock-Pot. I had to chase a cockroach out of my sock drawer. And maybe he was scared to disagree with me because of my crazy eyes and slight hysteria, but eventually he relented to the idea of giving me a little more time. He wouldn't put me in the hospital, but only if I agreed to do *exactly* as he ordered.

After a chest X-ray confirmed that I would survive a few more days hospital free, he gave me an ancient portable nebulizer and strict instructions to use it a gazillion times a day. It must have weighed like thirty-five pounds, but I was to carry it with me at all times and never, ever, *ever* miss a breathing treatment. His orders also included respiratory therapy to be administered by my husband at home, which he demonstrated by having me lie in certain prone positions and thumping my torso repeatedly with his hands cupped like paddles. As he thumped, he said, "Please tell your husband I want him to *pound you*, not spank you—there should be *no spanking*, and it is of the utmost importance you get a good pounding right before bed."

I am not even kidding.

Steve was able to come home that night, and between the mandatory poundings, a hearty antibiotic/steroid cocktail, and a number of actual cocktails, I felt alive and human again by the end of the week. It was such an effective course of treatment that, to this day, if I come down with even the slightest hint of a cough, I can count on a generous offer from Steve to give me a good pounding right before bed.

———

Strangely, the biggest surprise waiting for us in Costa Rica wasn't the language or the culture or the climate. It was, of all things, the missionaries.

Surprise! Sometime *missionaries* are *the worst.*

Who knew?!

Okay, lots of people already knew this, but I wasn't one of them.

13

The Butterfly Eater

Before we moved to Latin America, I'd met only a handful of missionaries. Of course, I'd heard all the old stereotypes and generalizations about how they can be kind of awkward or whatever, but the half dozen or so modern missionaries I'd met were fairly normal people with decent social skills. I assumed they were pretty standard as far as missionaries go.

Well, I assumed wrong.

The language school I attended during that first year turned out to be a mecca for newly commissioned missionaries who came to learn Spanish on their way to assignments in various other Latin American countries. And after several months of school days trapped in humid classrooms with a few of the most unlikable people I'd ever met, I decided there were three main types of missionary. The first was the kind I'd known—fairly regular people (with just enough of an odd streak to do something crazy like move overseas to serve

Jesus). The second was the kind we've all heard about—total weirdos with terrible interpersonal skills. But the third type (and, debatably, the most common) were self-righteous dickwads who honestly believed they were so amazing Jesus needed them to save the world.

To be fair, many of these enthusiastic new missionaries didn't know what to make of me and Steve either. We were the nondenominational, egalitarian beer drinkers. Steve had tattoos and I had a ring in my nose. All of this was taken by some as evidence that we were heathens in need of the gospel. The frequency with which we were evangelized by fellow students was almost hilarious. It didn't help that Steve kept making straight-faced jokes about our vast collection of Buddha statues, and that the rest of his wives would be arriving in a week.

Despite our differences, Steve and I grew fond of some of the other language-school missionaries. I can't even imagine what life would have looked like without the community and camaraderie we found alongside some of our compadres that year. Truly, if not for a few like-minded friends, we would have been totally alone on an island in a sea of *what the fuck*.

———

One day a group of us sat together in white plastic chairs around a white plastic table, in the shade of a covered patio, to lament our latest Spanish gaffes and expand on our life stories with new friends. We snacked on greasy empanadas and drank watery coffee out of Styrofoam cups while we talked, and on this particular day, someone set the remainder of a half-eaten banana in the middle of the table. It was all very normal. We were having a normal chat, like normal people who do normal things, when, drawn to the open banana, a soft white butterfly fluttered down into the center of our circle. A few of us continued to watch the pretty little visitor as it explored the fruit, and everyone returned to the conversation . . . that is, almost everyone.

This one guy suddenly leaned across the table with a scary intensity in his eye. He already had a reputation as kind of an oddball, but this was weird even for him. As we looked on, he inched his face closer and closer to the banana until his cheek almost brushed against it, and the butterfly, sensing his dangerous proximity, stopped moving. The man seemed to have arrived at his intended destination, because there he hovered while his mouth opened slowly, like a small pink cargo-bay door, and then, without warning, *he slurped up the butterfly.*

Like, he ate it.

It was gone.

The rest of us let out a round of gasps. My hands flew to my temples to keep my brain from exploding out of my head, and I screeched, *"WHAT DID YOU DO???"*

But he didn't even look up. With his cheeks puffed out, he leaned back in his chair, ever so slowly opened his creepy mouth once again, and stuck out his

tongue . . . and there it was: the butterfly. Clearly trau-
matized, but happy to be alive. After about three long,
terrible seconds perched on the end of a grown man's
tongue, it spread papery wings and flew away.

I exhaled. Phew! See? It's okay! He didn't *actually*
eat it, because . . . *no, seriously, can someone please tell
me what the hell just happened?!*

While we stared, the guy explained that he had
been conducting experiments on wildlife to see how
close you can get to another living creature with your
mouth versus with your hand. "You'd be amazed at
how many things will let you eat them," he said.

As if that were a perfectly reasonable thing to say
out loud.

Unable to further contain myself, I blurted out,
"That is the weirdest thing I've ever seen in my entire
life. *That's not normal.* You know you're not a scien-
tist, right? Like, you're just some random dude going
around *licking animals for fun!*"

A week later, I glanced out the window at school
during a test on subjunctive phrases, and there was the
Butterfly Eater in the bright morning sun. His khaki
chinos were way too short, his striped polo was way too
long, and he was chasing a lizard in circles around the
trunk of a date palm with his mouth.

Come on, now. How did *that guy* end up a missionary in a foreign country? The question begged to be
asked. How did this happen? Had he too been "called
by God" to do awesome and amazing things?

Let me be clear. I am *not* saying God couldn't or

didn't use the Butterfly Eater to bring light or joy or goodness to some quirky souls out there in the great big world. These questions had less to do with the people themselves and more to do with a system that paves the way for anyone who feels like it to move to a foreign country, and then gives them permission to do virtually whatever they please under the loosely defined title "missionary."

During our time at language school, we traded stories about how we'd become missionaries. Reports ranged from "I lost my job and didn't have any good prospects, so God called me to the mission field" to "I was on a luxury cruise that stopped at a gorgeous port city in Central America, and I loved it so much God laid it on my heart to move there." We met people who'd been dreaming of missionary life since the time they were twelve years old and experienced the thrill of handing out sack lunches to inner-city homeless on a church field trip. We met others who'd never considered missions until four months ago, when, while watching a *NatGeo* documentary on the History Channel, they discovered a passion for barefoot llama herders in the mountains of Peru. Our group contained hipsters and grandmas, pastors and plumbers, CEOs and college kids, cops and stay-at-home moms, and we were all there because, essentially, *we felt like it*. At some point, in one way or another, we had each concluded we'd been called by God, and so, apparently, *we were*.

But was that enough?

Would "God's calling" and a year of language school make an electrician capable of running an orphanage? Prepare a high school teacher to plant a church or a youth pastor to start a business in a new place and culture? Was it enough to turn people like me into—oh, I don't know—functional adults? I know this sounds mean, but looking around at the crowd I was running with, I began to have serious doubts.

I do believe that God *can* use anyone to do anything (that I am writing this book is a prime example), but I was beginning to see how that is a pretty weak standard by which to choose whom we send out into the world to "be the hands and feet of Jesus," or whatever you want to call it. This isn't about having unrealistic expectations of ordinary people, and it's not about negating God's ability to surprise us by doing amazing things. It's about recognizing that we have a responsibility, as the church, to *choose* whom we send, so that we send the right people to do the right things in the right places—and to *not send them* when it's not right.

And therein lies the real problem: There's really not much choosing going on. If you raise your hand (and have enough cash), someone *will* send you out. I like to call this the Butterfly Eater Effect.

I'm gonna let you in on a little trade secret: Nobody wants to tell anyone they shouldn't be a missionary—not even the butterfly eaters. It's practically against the rules. In fact, if you even try to suggest that an aspiring missionary may not be a good fit for the work, the life-style, or the region he or she feels called to, you better be prepared for the spiritual flogging of a lifetime.

Who are you to say what God can do through them?!

God loves to use unlikely people to blah blah blah!

Look at Moses! Look at Rahab! Look at Jesus! Look at that one guy with no arms and legs! Look at how God used them!

Unfortunately, those who champion the current method do not want you to *actually* look at Moses. They're not interested in discussing how Moses was especially groomed and prepared by his early life within the Egyptian royal court to be the one person in all the land who could successfully lead a stand against his adoptive bro, the pharaoh. They do not want to talk about how, in addition to being a successful prostitute, Rahab was a keen, self-sufficient businesswoman who was uniquely situated—not just because of her snazzy apartment but also because of her kick-ass *personality*—to be a hero. Oh, and Jesus? Literally *born* to do what he did for the world. Moreover, the Bible tells us that Jesus handpicked the first disciples and "selected" the seventy-some pairs of missionaries he sent out. Like, he *chose* them from among a larger group of people he'd been teaching for months.

Unlike Jesus, I may not know what you were born to do, but if you're a grown man who doesn't make eye contact and picks his nose and eats it while using public transportation, I'm gonna go ahead and suggest that maybe you *not* go live overseas and call yourself a missionary. And I won't even feel bad about it.

———

When I told Steve about the Butterfly Eater, we laughed and groaned and threw our hands up in the air. But it turns out, we'd both been mulling over similar concerns for the past few months, and I think it was Steve who finally said it out loud. "What if that guy's not here because he was 'called by God'? What if he's here because the system is broken?"

It was a frightening question, because if the Butterfly Eater had made it all the way to Costa Rica by slipping through the cracks, *then maybe we had too.* In the process that led us there, we had often been advised, "God doesn't call the equipped. He equips the called." We had practically congratulated ourselves for being inexperienced and unqualified for the work ahead. But surrounded by a whole bunch of other unqualified/ill-equipped missionaries, I began to question this logic.

Didn't saying God doesn't call the equipped but equips the called imply that equipping comes to us in a single, romantic instant in which we are suddenly transformed into someone more skilled and more capable than before? Because that didn't seem to be happening for any of us. I wondered if, in clinging to the idea that God's equipping *follows* God's calling, we have flooded the planet with Christian do-gooders who may, for any number of reasons, be unfit, incompetent, or just plain unnecessary. And I wondered if I was one of them.

But what if God has been preparing us—*equipping us*—since the day we were born? What if all of our experiences, good and bad, beautiful and terrible, Christian and not-so-Christian, have a role in preparing us for the next step in our journey? Like, what if our character traits, life skills, personality, and education *are* the equipping?

In that first year in our tropical paradise, Steve and I would lie in bed in the dark, listening to the geckos above our heads chirp like smoke detectors in need of fresh batteries, talking about the broken system and butterfly eaters in hushed tones, as if we'd uncovered the kind of scandal that could get us killed in our sleep.

14
The Very Worst Year

To say that our second year in Costa Rica was the worst year of my life sounds *so dramatic*, and I'm afraid you'll be disappointed when you hear that it was actually pretty boring. I'm not about to confess a sordid Latin love affair or detail a maiming accident or anything like that. No one died. No one lost a limb. No one got a divorce. The truth is, the things that happened in my very worst year aren't even the worst things that have ever happened to me. But it wasn't the actual events that made it so bad; it was the constant feeling of ineptitude and shame that swept over my head like a rogue wave that never receded.

I'd come into this whole missionary gig with a comprehensive plan for guaranteed success:

1. Show up.
2. Learn Spanish.
3. Kick ass.

I really thought that if I went to all the trouble of becoming a missionary, those three things would come together as easily as mixing a cocktail. Dead serious. I believed in this magical three-part formula for a happy life overseas, and I assumed God would hand it over like a cosmic Moscow mule. After language school, it was time for me to finally get down to business making Costa Rican friends, settling my family into a home, and learning the pace of my new job. I was ready to drink deeply of God's special blessing, ready to receive my prize for becoming a missionary.

But then the funniest thing happened. Parts one, two, and three of my perfect plan for success sort of just *fell apart* . . . and I sort of fell apart too.

I'm going tell you what happened, but be fore-warned. This is a whiny story, and you're probably going to think I'm a total wiener with no perspective, because my very worst year was, like, ten million times better than some people's very best years. I know this. Bear with me, please, as I share how my expectations of awesomeness eroded, and try to remember that this all went down at the same time. It would be easy to say, "Our house was a disaster, friendship was scarce, and the job I'd come to do didn't actually exist"—just, like, a checklist of huge bummers. But to do so fails to achieve the chronic sense of piling on. It fails to depict how some days were nearly slapstick in nature, with all of our problems crashing together, setting each other off, bouncing against one another, until our whole family fell into bed at night overwhelmed, undone, and miserable.

———

We started our second year by moving out of a tiny old house and into a big, fancy, new place in the suburbs of Heredia. We'd made arrangements to house-sit this really nice house for some other missionaries while they were in the United States for a year. I joked about how we'd given up everything we owned in exchange for a simple life as humble servants, only to be blessed by God with the nicest house we would ever live in. But secretly I kinda thought that was true. God was finally rewarding us for our sacrifice by making our new life a tiny bit luxurious, tossing in a dishwasher and maid's quarters for good measure. A gourmet kitchen, three and a half bathrooms, and a full-size hot water tank were all just a little nod to us from the creator of the universe for a job well done.

For the record, the Bible *does* make us promises about what happens when we get serious about following Jesus. It tells us it's gonna suck. It will be difficult and uncomfortable and costly. But somehow I'd convinced myself that *for me* God would make an exception. So you can imagine my disappointment when the amazing house that I believed was the Lord's special gift turned out to be a life-sucking vortex of despair.

The odor was the first bad omen.

Right after we moved in, we noticed that as you

rounded the top of the stairs into the loft, you'd occasionally be hit in the face with what seemed like the stench of a dead body. The homeowners said they knew about the problem and had looked everywhere for a cause, even hiring someone to explore the nooks and crannies of the roof for animal remains, but they never found the culprit. I actually wish it had been a dead animal, because the smell of a rotting corpse would have eventually dissipated, but not this. The stench came and went a few times each week for the entire time we lived there, testing our gag reflexes and forcing us to reassure disgusted houseguests that, no, we were not making a massive batch of kimchi in the upstairs bathtub.

Then the walls started to leak. Like, all of sudden, water would just start pouring out of a wall. The walls leaked steadily in the kitchen and in the kids' bathroom. One night I woke up to find a pool of water creeping across our bedroom floor, because the wall behind the master bathroom vanity also decided to spring a leak. A puddle that appeared in the middle of the living room indicated yet another leak, this time conveniently located between the first and second floors.

The house, like most in Costa Rica, was built from cinder blocks and rebar, which makes fixing plumbing problems a huge effing pain in the ass. You have to figure out exactly where the leak is (it may not be where the water is coming through), then hand-chisel through plaster and cement block, replace the pipe, and patch it all up again. This process required hours of hard labor and mental energy, and we were in short supply of both. By *we* I mean Steve. (Please. I don't know how to, like, *do things*.) He did his best to keep the gushers plugged, but with Steve's workload, we finally agreed that some of the smaller leaks just wouldn't get fixed until the owners came back. We would have to live with them.

So in that big, dreamy kitchen of black granite and stainless steel, the walls seeped in unreachable places and puddles collected beneath the built-in cupboards. The permanent musty smell of stagnant water combined on occasion with the wretched stink of decomposing flesh wafting down from the loft.

Home, sweet home.

As an additional kick to the nuts, on a sunny Sunday morning, while we were at church like a good missionary family, someone broke in and stole all of our stuff.

We felt vulnerable and violated, but we were able to shrug off the loss of all the material things except a hard drive that held about two years' worth of family photos. It was the burglary itself that was so deeply hurtful—as though the welcome mat to our new life had officially been pulled out from under us.

It didn't help that the people we believed responsible for the theft worked directly across the street and could watch us come and go. We got to see them nearly every single time we locked up and left the house, wondering if it would still be locked when we returned. The break-in made us all uneasy, insecure, and distrustful of the house where we so badly wanted to feel at home.

Living in a foreign country is a hundred thousand times more draining than doing your regular life in your native country. At the end of those long days, my family needed a place of rest more than ever, but what we had was a stinky, leaky, distressing place to lay our heads at night. That stupid house may have been pretty, but it was never home.

———

After the burglary, I could feel myself slipping into a depression I'd been able to stave off for years through medication, exercise, and counseling. Still, in the same way I thought God had blessed me with that fancy house, I secretly expected God to protect me from mental illness. I assumed that because I'd *just showed up*, God would grant me immunity, even from my own self.

Though I could scarcely drag myself out of bed in the morning and I dreaded the idea of going outside, I decided that all I really needed to do was get back into a good, solid exercise routine and eat healthy.

I still don't know why I thought this was a good idea.

Running outdoors in Costa Rica came with a whole new set of challenges. The sidewalks are mossy and unpredictable, with deep holes (lovingly referred to as "gringo traps") that appear out of nowhere. Stray dogs roam the streets, often in mangy gangs, dotting the terrain with a minefield of poop nuggets. But the worst part is the relentless stream of whistling, catcalls, and marriage proposals from grown men hanging halfway out of car windows to let you know how thrilled they are to see that you put on your stretchy pants and left the house that day. I was never quite sure if I was being genuinely hit on or openly mocked. I came home early from nearly every attempt at a run, embarrassed and wary and wishing I were invisible, and the idea of regular exercise quickly lost its appeal.

Despite the abundance of cheap regional fruits and veggies, eating well proved just as challenging for me. I am sincerely the laziest person I've ever met, and aside from bananas, the tropics are not exactly overflowing with healthy food for lazy people. I don't know if you know this, but tropical fruit is like *super labor-intensive*. Mango requires a knife, passion fruit a spoon, and if you want a coconut, you better have a machete handy. Through the lethargy of depression, cutting a pineapple seemed impossibly hard. And, yes, papaya *is* easy to prepare, but it tastes like a big toe and a butthole had a baby, so no thank you. It was much easier for me to keep reaching for prepackaged garbage food like cookies and chips and pastries. So while the plan had been to improve my physical health in order to improve my mental health, in the end it was like the two of them teamed up and decided to go down with the ship together.

I grew more depressed. And also I grew a muffin top.

In the middle of the day, you could usually find me at home in my pajamas eating *queque seco* with my fingers and drinking yesterday's coffee while I surfed the Internet for recipes for comfort foods I could make from scratch; corn dogs, bagels, berry pie. I had a few good friends to hang out with—mostly other missionaries from our team—and there was a weekly women's Bible study to attend, so it's not like I was a complete shut-in. I had a social life and regular commitments, but if there was even a hint of a reason for me to skip out, I'd grab it. Staying in pajamas and sucking down stale coffee seemed so doable compared to the hard work of language learning and culture grasping and relationship building.

A few of us put together a weekly kids' club for the youngsters from one of the area's most impoverished neighborhoods. We brought fresh bread and ripe bananas to fill their hungry bellies and a Bible lesson with a coloring page or some kind of messy craft for their busy little hands. One day I was standing in the pouring rain, trying to hail a taxi on my way out to the shantytown where we held the club. The rain got heavier, soaking my pants up to the knees, and still, no taxi. Finally my cell phone buzzed and, much to my relief, I learned the kids' club had been called off because no one was likely to show up. I was so happy to turn around and head back to my warm, dry hiding place, so glad to avoid speaking Spanish, so thrilled to climb back into my PJs. I thanked God for a rainfall so heavy it kept the kids home. Yes. The underclothed, malnourished, needy kids I was supposed to love would be stuck in their shacks, with a bedsheet for a front door, a plastic bowl and cooking pot to catch the water drizzling in through holes in a rusty roof, and a handful of rice and beans for a meal, and I *thanked God*.

Because *clearly* there was something very wrong with me. That's what depression does. It clouds your vision, it turns you inward, and it makes it very hard for you to see beyond yourself.

The thing is, whenever I bothered to shower and dress and get where I needed to be, I was always glad I did. I had some amazing people in my life, people I enjoyed and loved being with, people who encouraged me and laughed with me and made me feel less alone. I felt pleased with myself after I went around town paying bills and attending to business in Spanish like a real grown-up. And the truth is, I loved working with those kids every week. They were often grimy, bratty, and unappreciative—regular kids—but I sincerely loved them and wanted to be with them. Whether it was to catch the bus heading up the mountain or a taxi into the city or simply to stroll to the corner store for milk, I felt better when I faced the day and made the walk up the hill from my house into society. That active, capable, confident woman was the woman I wanted to be!

But depression is a sneaky son of a bitch. It creeps

in behind your joy to convince you that to live a life you love isn't worth the effort. It whispers and lies and manipulates, and pretty soon you're certain that the hill from your house to the rest of the world is just too damn steep.

———

Trust me, I know how lame this sounds. You're probably rolling your eyes so hard right now, like, *Aw, Jamie, you poor thing. You had to smell a bad smell and cut a pineapple all by yourself? You had to* walk *up a hill? How did you ever survive such trials and tribulations???*

I know. *I know.* These were not exactly Job-level catastrophes. But the problem wasn't that any of these things happened—it was that they were all happening at once. It could turn into a comedy of errors.

Like this: When the paralysis of depression kept me from paying the bills on time, the power would inevitably get shut off on a day we were expecting a dozen visiting North Americans for dinner. I would lose three hours (which I'd planned to use cooking and cleaning) getting into town to pay the electric bill. On the way home from the bank, a toothless drunk on the street would grope me, and while trying to escape Mr. Grabby Hands, I'd slip in dog shit and stumble into a ditch full of refuse. While I was gone, Steve would come home for lunch to find the power out *again* and a new wall spring gushing into the dining room. Then I'd return, smelling like a turd rolled in trash, to find him elbows deep in plumbing repairs, on top of a pile of rubble, with a thin layer of cinder-block dust covering every surface in the house. It would take a herculean effort from both of us to get the power back on, the leak stopped, the house cleaned, and a decent meal prepared, which by some miracle we would get done five minutes before our company arrived.

Feeling victorious over the disaster of this day, Steve and I would high-five each other as we swaggered out to the street to greet our dinner guests . . . only to find that our car had been stolen.

Hi. Hello. Welcome to my life.

It was like that *all the time.* Nothing ever happened that was so crazy or devastating we felt like we needed to pack up and leave, but the relentlessness of it all exhausted us.

But here's the thing. We still believed we were there for the right reasons—and a person can put up with a lot of crap for a long time when it's for a good reason.

People stay in terrible jobs for decades simply because that job provides for their family. A parent will sacrifice desperately needed sleep to care for a sick child night after night. People endure the torture of chemotherapy for the chance to love and be loved here on earth a little while longer. Women go through the ache of labor and the agony of pushing a basketball out of their hoo-ha to bring little human beings into the world. And do you know why we do all that? *Because it's worth it.* The human spirit can and will endure incredible things—humiliation, hardship, unimaginable pain, and relentless suffering—if there's a purpose.

Steve and I became missionaries because, in a fantastic leap of altruistic faith, we believed it would be worth it. We uprooted our family, disrupted our boys' childhood, and upended our entire future not just because God asked us to but because we actually thought maybe God had something important for us to do in Costa Rica. We could live in a house that smelled like a swampy graveyard, we could deal with all of our stuff getting stolen, we could work through the isolation and the loneliness and the depression—as long as we believed God had an actual *purpose* for us there.

The worst part of the worst year of my life was a growing realization that perhaps none of it actually mattered. As a missionary, I had a meaningful-sounding title, but it didn't really matter if I never left the house. No one questioned what I did or didn't do, so it didn't make a difference if I did or didn't get dressed every day. I could stay home in my pajamas and write a Facebook update about the weather, and I'd get ten comments in five minutes telling me how brave/awesome/exceptional/*amazing* I was for being there and how lucky Costa Rica was to have me.

That was the worst part.

I showed up believing I was called, expecting to be equipped and hoping to change lives, only to learn that Costa Rica didn't really need another missionary. Turns out they already had gobs of their own churches and pastors and spiritual leaders—they had Bible colleges and seminaries, for fuck's sake. Costa Rican

Christians didn't need North American Christians to teach them how to follow Jesus, and Costa Rican people didn't need any more well-intentioned foreigners to come and "help" them. They were just fine before we got there, and they'd be just fine when we left.

I showed up believing that Costa Rica needed me and that God would use me, but when I looked around at that beautiful country, at my hardworking neighbors, at the thriving church, I could only wonder, *For what?*

God only knew.

No, but really, I think He did.

15

Friday-Night Lights

After the very worst year, we moved into a humble little house in a small neighborhood surrounded by coffee fields on all sides. Unlike the fancy-shmancy stinker of a house, this place didn't have a water heater or a dishwasher or a push-button garage door with a clicker in the car. The powder room downstairs was so small Steve couldn't stand upright without hitting his head on the ceiling or sit down without jamming both knees into the wall. There were heavy bars on all of the windows, and a big fat lock and chain secured the iron gate outside a dinky carport.

Like many of the suburban neighborhoods in Costa Rica, this was a gated community, so everyone had to enter and leave past a tiny guard shack at the front entrance, where a uniformed man with a rusty revolver tucked into the waistband of his pants walked the barricade open and shut. With the front secured, another guard would "patrol" the streets by bicycle about once an hour, blowing a whistle at regular intervals to let people know he was out there, diligently protecting their property.

When Steve and I first went to have a look, a friendly neighbor met us outside with the keys. She let us in and started to show us around, but then she stopped abruptly, saying in Spanish, "Do you like dogs?"

We looked at each other and shrugged. "Yeah, dogs are cool."

She said, "Wait right here!"

We watched her run back across the street to her house and return holding a bundle, and then she plopped the sweetest, cutest, fluffiest puppy I'd ever seen into my arms. Grinning, she said, "I thought you might like to hold her while you look around—she's looking for a home too."

A little black ball of fur gazed up at me with big brown eyes, and it was obvious this lady was trying to sucker us into taking that puppy off her hands. I honestly couldn't think of a worse idea than taking on a dog at that point, so I held the fluff bucket out at arm's length, preparing a proper rejection in my head. I made a show of looking the dog over critically, and then I said, "Ooooooooohhhh, shmoopy-whoopy-pwecious-poopy-pie, I wuv you, yesh I do! We'll take her!"

Steve stared at me, his head cocked and his lips pressed tightly together like, *Why did you do that???*

About two weeks after we moved in, our little pup was weaned and ready to join us, but when I went to

get her from the neighbor, she was pouncing and playing with the rest of her roly-poly littermates, and it
broke my heart to think of her all alone at our house. I
couldn't bear the thought of being the one to tear that
little baby away from her whole doggy family. I just
couldn't do it! So instead of bringing home a puppy? I
brought home *two* puppies.

Steve still hasn't forgiven me, but the kids were
thrilled.

We named the super chill little bear of a dog Osita,
which means "little bear," and we called the other one,
who was golden blond, high maintenance, and always
causing trouble, Gringa, which (more or less) means
"white chick."

I don't know if you know this, but puppies are a
pretty good reason to get up in the morning. Mostly
because they're cute and funny and ridiculously happy
to see you, but also because, if you don't get up and
tend to them, they'll eat, shred, and shit on everything
you own. I'm not gonna pretend those energetic balls of
love cured my depression, but they helped an awful lot.

Those two puppies and that humble little house
in a small neighborhood surrounded by coffee fields
breathed new life into me.

For the first time in a long time, I felt like I might
be *home*.

It might not have had hot water, but with the exception of the teeny half bathroom tucked under the stairs,
natural light reached into every corner of the house.

The new place was half the size, but sharing a wall on either side with the neighbors had made the old house feel dark and caveish, more like a place to hide from life than a place to live in. Situated on a corner, with windows on three sides and a sunny backyard, our new home felt vibrant and alive, and while it couldn't be described as a house with great views, you didn't have to go far to find them. Not twenty steps from the front gate, I could stand and watch the morning mist pour over the top of our mountain to roll down across acres of coffee, shaded by avocado and banana trees. Just a few houses down, an empty lot full of tall grass and weeds made the perfect spot to watch Turrialba, the nearest active volcano, belching impressive plumes of smoke and ash into the sky. Even the carpenter ants were charming, snipping foliage and flowers from nearby trees and marching down the street holding their bounty above their heads in a miniature parade. You just couldn't watch them disappear into the ground without wondering whose party they were decorating for.

The neighborhood brimmed with activity, and it was like the house itself stuck out into a world I'd grown good at ignoring. Now I was forced to take notice.

During the day, sounds from the street filled the kitchen, which is where I spent most of my time, because food. Obviously. The neighbor's talking parrot chatted endlessly with no one, squawking his owner's name, "Farah," mimicking the *tweet tweet tweet* of the guard's whistle, or just calling out, *"¡Hola, lorito!"* (Hello, parrot!) again and again and again. The conversations of the coffee pickers who used our road as a shortcut to get from one field to the next, with big round baskets slung over their shoulders, drifted indoors, as did the shouts of door-to-door salesmen walking down the middle of the street with their carts full of goodies: brooms, garden tools, VHS tapes, air fresheners depicting Catholic icons, and plastic baggies filled with mystery cleaning fluids. Since I was often home during the day, they would sometimes stop at my open kitchen window, tapping the iron fence to get my attention. *"Machita,"* they would call inside. "Brooms! Come see the brooms! Low prices!" In the morning sunshine, young mamas and old grannies pushed babies in strollers around and around the block while they gossiped on their cell phones. And at any given time, at least one neighbor would be playing a radio or watching a telenovela loud enough to be heard by all.

In the afternoon the street would grow quiet and still, as every living thing made itself scarce before puffy clouds from both sides of the valley met overhead and thunder and lightning cracked the sky open. Rain came down in sheets against the windows, creating a watercolor mosaic out of familiar images—all the bits of life that I'd seen so clearly not five minutes before, now beautifully out of focus.

I loved the rain.

Rain in Costa Rica is one of those things that's impossible to understand unless you've experienced it for yourself. It's, like, *more rainy* than regular rain; bigger, stronger, wetter, even. It doesn't just fall; it's driven. It hits the earth with almost unnatural force, and once on land, it doesn't run; it rages. Above ground the rain collects to lift and steal anything untethered, dragging it away. And underground it gathers power, rushing to return to the river, the stream, the ocean, where it patiently waits its turn to become the rain again.

Rain can be destructive and dangerous. It can make you miserable. But you can't live without it, and you wouldn't want to, because after the rain stops, the world around you is better for it—fresher, lusher, greener, cleaner, and more alive. Maybe this sounds silly, but when the rain comes in Costa Rica, it's like it comes to teach you a lesson.

I especially loved the rain on garbage day, when we all piled our plastic sacks of trash on the curb to be picked up and earnestly prayed for the trash collectors to get to these piles before twenty stray dogs did. But inevitably, by 9:00 a.m. the street would be littered with moldy rice, dry chicken bones, fermented fruit rinds, smashed black beans, and every kind of rubbish. This made for a field day for cockroaches and other vermin, but a good hard rain would save us, washing away the rotten remains of a long week and leaving us with a clean slate.

That's what the new house felt like to me. It didn't just look brighter; it felt lighter, like the air after a heavy rainfall. It was like a fresh start after my internal garbage had gotten out of hand. A clean slate after a very long, very messy year.

———

Around that time, one of the guys we knew started playing football. Not Latin American *fútbol* but, like, *football* football—pads, helmets, tackling, touchdowns—*North American football.* Knowing Steve had played in college, our friend asked if he would come out to watch his team practice, which of course Steve was happy to do. And that's how he learned about the new semipro football league that had recently made its way into parks, plazas, and soccer pitches scattered around the provinces. With only a handful of teams, the league was heavily recruiting for more players and coaches.

Surely you see where this is going. . . .

In his usual fashion, Steve jumped in with both feet. He first joined the league as an assistant coach, and then, when his team needed more bodies for eligibility, he became a player too.

When people say, "God's plans are more amazing than anything you could ever imagine for yourself!" I think maybe this is the kind of thing they're talking about. When Steve was playing college ball, neither of us would have dreamed that someday he would find his way back onto the field, coaching in a foreign country and in a second language. (That would have been a pretty weird dream, if we're being honest.) But doesn't it actually make perfect sense that Steve's path would lead him to football in Costa Rica in a super practical way? I mean, even though it seems like the most impossible, unlikely thing, doesn't it follow that as we go about serving God, we would gravitate toward the things we're *already* equipped, educated, and naturally gifted to do?

It was the last thing we expected, but the best thing. The football community expanded our circle of friends way beyond the Christian missionary bubble. Awkward as it was, we were open with the other coaches and players about Steve's day job, explaining that we had indeed come to Costa Rica as missionaries (he was still busting ass on the ministry campus at least five days a week, so it's not like it was a secret). While the Christian community tends to blindly revere missionaries, we'd noticed that other people seemed a bit more skeptical and, well, weirded out by them. And as we got to know the players better, some of the guys were brutally honest with us about how both long- and short-term missionaries were often perceived by locals, and that was as lazy, spoiled, entitled, patronizing, and just plain annoying. By now this wasn't exactly a shock to us.

To their credit, our new Costa Rican friends easily forgave the naïveté and arrogance that had dropped us on their doorstep, and our relationships with the players and their wives and girlfriends were refreshingly free of the awkwardness and distrust that the word "missionary" brings to the table. With their gracious acceptance, we made our way into a community of real human beings who talked in normal words, said what they meant, asked good questions, challenged our perceptions, and shared their opinions based on personal experience and stark reality. I can't begin to tell you how exciting this was after enduring so much spiritual gobbledygook in the la-la land of churchianity.

Soon I could count on a full house for dinner a few nights a week, as players dropped in to share a meal or just hang out. Sometimes we ended up singing folk songs and dancing salsa after filling up on *salchichón*, *carne asada*, and *micheladas*, but more often than not, our friends stayed late into the night to talk about life, and faith, and following Jesus.

On the football field and hanging out late, Steve escaped the ball and chain of his day job. There he was just Coach: a leader, a teammate, and a brother. Without ulterior motive, he got to know his players well and looked for ways to encourage and support them both on and off the field. Watching all this play out, I started to understand something I'd failed to grasp before we became professional missionaries: Our calling is not what we do as much as it is who we are while we do it.

In one night game on a makeshift field in San José, Steve was playing defensive line for the first time in nearly two decades. Seeing him in full pads and a helmet, I sincerely worried that my husband was too rusty and old to be out there, but about five minutes into the game, I realized my concern was unnecessary. On the field Steve had natural size on his side, plus skills and years of experience. He'd be fine.

But the other spectators chattering in Spanish, trying to figure out the rules of a new sport, were a constant reminder that this was a different time and place. Uprights were fashioned from lengths of PVC pipe held to the vertical posts of existing soccer goals with zip ties and prayer. They swayed in the breeze that ruffled through a forest of banana trees just beyond the end zone. At the snack bar, a hamburger included a slice of limp deli ham (because Costa Rica), and a syrupy shaved ice came with a layer of powdered milk in the middle and sweetened condensed milk drizzled on top (see ham note). I sat down to watch the game with a paper plate of mushy french fries and a Coke Light from a bottle, which had been thoughtfully opened and poured into a plastic bag tightly knotted around a straw, and nothing says "We're not in Kansas anymore!" like holding a sack of warm soda.

After the first play, I anxiously watched Steve peel himself off a pile of bodies on the field, as I had so many times so many years ago. And I was amused to suddenly realize that I knew precisely what came next. He would give another player a hand up, then he would tighten the Velcro on the backs of his gloves and, casually flipping his mouth guard with his front teeth, rest his hands on his hips to catch his breath while the refs conferred—which is *exactly* what happened. And just as I had in a different lifetime, I had taken my place in the stands above the fifty-yard line, where I sat washed out in the glare of stadium lights, chilled from the butt up by an aluminum bleacher seat, lamenting that I'd gone with fries instead of nachos. It was all so different, and all so exactly the same.

See, God has this weird habit of bringing our lives around full circle, so that things we thought we'd forgotten, the stuff we thought was behind us, even the history we fear will always define us, can become the very thing we use to bring others into the fold, recycling the fabric of our lives into some form of redemption.

That football season, I came home one day to find a giant pile of smelly football gear waiting for my attention. Jerseys needed to be washed and folded, helmets and shoulder pads needed a heavy dose of disinfectant, and the water jugs needed a good rinse before it could all be packed into the back of our clunky Hyundai Galloper to be hauled out to the field for the weekend game.

As I sorted everything into piles, then loaded the washer, I had to hold my nose to keep from gagging. But I found myself smiling, because the whole scenario was so damn funny. We had come to Costa Rica with our sights set on Sunday-morning programs, but God was using us for bigger things under Friday-night lights.

PART 4

Fix It, Jesus

16

The Scales Fall

I don't know if you ever noticed this, but football players aren't usually built like soccer players. They're usually a lot bigger (and by "bigger" I mean fatter). That said, the introduction of North American football to the area shone like a beacon of hope for Central America's, ahem, *larger* athletes. Finally there was a local sport for big-boned, lumbering lard-ass brothers—a place for the bulky guy with a healthy competitive edge who'd been sized off the soccer field since fifth grade. Of course, football attracted all kinds of well-rounded jocks, but American football flipped the script in Costa Rica. A lean, fast running back could always be recruited right off a soccer pitch, but now a big beefy lineman was a truly hot commodity.

Our players came from all walks of life. They were college students, mechanics, engineers, salesmen, musicians, real estate agents, sports bookies, pizza couriers, IT guys, and customer service reps. A handful of them worked for U.S.-based companies like Microsoft, Sprint, and FedEx. One guy might show up to practice with his own gear in the trunk of a shiny German sports car, and another might have had to take three buses to get there, then rummage for shoulder pads and a helmet in the pile of communal equipment owned by the team. But these differences quickly disappeared beneath the solidarity of the jersey.

In the love our players developed for one another, the spirit of belonging they shared, and the promise of community that comes with being part of a team, the little world of Costa Rican semipro football felt in many ways like a church. Steve and I discovered that the growing connection and increasing intimacy we had within our football family felt more alive and meaningful than any part of the "work" we were doing on campus as so-called missionaries.

Still, we hesitated to call any part of our involvement with the team "ministry." We'd seen a lot of missionaries refer to the people in their lives as "opportunities" and "undertakings," talking about them in monthly newsletters the way you'd talk about renovating your bathroom. *I've spent many hours with Maribél, and after investing in her for months, I feel like it's starting to pay off. God willing, soon she's really gonna shine!* Even the hired help (nannies, maids, gardeners) often turned into pawns in the game of making everything look incredibly spiritual and eternally significant, as they were regularly identified as the oh-so-grateful recipients of hand-me-downs, financial gifts, invitations to church, and unsolicited prayers.

To see some of these interactions firsthand and then come across the subsequent retelling of the moment for the benefit of supporters was a lesson in Missionary Manipulation 101. A missionary could say "God bless you" to the sneeze of a mere acquaintance with a head cold while they were out buying bread, and hours later you might find the very same incident, retold on Facebook, looking an awful lot like a heroic step in the direction of a man's salvation. *Had a wonderful opportunity to pray with my dear friend Luis the baker. He's been fighting illness and was so grateful when I stopped in the middle of a busy day for a moment of prayerful intercession on his behalf. #Blessed*

True? Pretty much.

Misleading? Abso-fuckin'-lutely.

I have to admit, I had used such tactics on occasion. I'd chosen from a selection of vague vocabulary to humbly suggest that anything and everything we touched was #blessed by our presence. When we spent time with Christians, we were "making disciples," and when we crossed paths with non-Christians, we were "planting seeds." Either way, *we* were the ones God was using, and *they* were the ones who needed it. The gross imbalance in this power dynamic never occurred to me, until one day when I heard another missionary talking to Steve about what a great opportunity the football team was and how (despite the fact that he knew *nothing* about football) he'd love to "get in on it." When he called the team a "missions gold mine" and "ripe for the picking," I thought that if our football players heard anyone talking about them like that, *I would die.*

These were our *friends*, and whether or not they wanted or needed to know Jesus was not something we were going to exploit for a paycheck or a newsletter. No way. The details of our personal relationships would not find their way onto the Internet or into a newsletter, couched in the mystery language of missions.

Steve's connection to football would help us to see many new truths about the muddy intersection of the church and the world.

A few months into Steve's first season with the team, they went out to participate in a sports clinic hosted by a Christian athletic ministry from the States. The group would donate used football gear and a few hours of specialized instruction in exchange for the opportunity to evangelize. Every team in the league agreed to this deal from these complete strangers because they needed the gear, and extra training was always helpful. On the morning of the event, though, this is what Steve witnessed: Local coaches and players who'd attended the same clinic the year before took a few minutes ahead of time to solicit *volunteers* to accept Jesus as their Lord and Savior. On our team of fifty, the head coach assigned a half dozen guys to raise their hands at the appointed time. Everyone else was urged to play along but not overdo it, so that the missionaries would feel successful and keep coming back.

After practice, the guys were asked to huddle up and take a seat on the grass. Right on cue, a couple of enthusiastic short-term missionaries got up to share their personal testimonies through a translator. They wrapped things up with an altar call, imploring everyone to bow their heads and close their eyes and asking anyone who felt led to "invite Jesus into his heart" to raise a hand. None of our players actually invited Jesus into their heart that day, but six brown hands shot up into the air, and everyone left happy.

Later, knowing we were still technically missionaries, our friends playfully teased us about the incident and pointed out that "our kind" would continue to be welcomed with open arms, because we always brought free stuff and because we funneled so much money, by way of tourism, into the country, year after year. They said missionaries could be counted on like arms dealers to smuggle any manner of American merchandise, undeclared, through customs and immigration. If it meant they could get out of paying Costa Rica's astronomical import tax on helmets, pads, cleats, and whatever else they needed, and if it created jobs for their friends and neighbors, our guys would *gladly* pretend to become Christians annually and bend over for a condescending pat on the head from a few well-meaning North American do-gooders.

"It's mutual exploitation," explained Mateo, who

worked for Intel and played tight end. "Everybody wins."

Caught between these two worlds, Steve and I felt conflicted. It was great to see the teams getting resources and support. But we knew those missionaries were gonna go back to their home churches and celebrate a false account of changed lives. They'd share pictures and tell stories and talk about how "blessed" a bunch of underprivileged third-world football players were to receive pads and helmets and practice jerseys. All the churchy people who wrote checks and stayed home would feel good, and when they heard how many guys committed their lives to Jesus, they'd pop a spiritual boner. They'd gladly send a group back to Costa Rica the next year, ostensibly to hold a football clinic but really (*wink wink*) to "build relationships" and "love on people."

Yeesh.

—

I'd begun to see a similar scenario playing out in the community I mentioned earlier, where some friends and I put on a weekly kids' club. The Precario, which amounted to an expanse of shacks on a muddy hillside, had become a regular destination for short-termers. They usually arrived with garbage bags full of used clothes and shoes, performed a puppet show or a skit, and handed out loads of candy.

Whenever a short-term team arrived, the Precario

mothers sent all of their youngsters, because they knew their kids could play gringos like a fiddle. Older boys and girls would run to greet these missionaries with huge smiles on their dirty little faces, while younger siblings held back, giving the foreigners something to work for. The kids marveled at cameras and cell phones, as if they'd never seen either before in their whole entire life, happily climbing onto complete strangers' laps for selfies and grinning for photo ops. But the really clever kids stood apart from the group, looking forlorn and doe-eyed, until one of the anguished suburbanites singled them out for special attention. Before the hour was up, that kid was usually wearing a new bracelet or carrying the new key chain they'd begged off their empathetic benefactor.

Waving like crazy through the windows of their rental van, the group would leave, delightfully heartbroken, feeling like they'd done something special to touch the lives of needy kids in an exotic country. As soon as they found Wi-Fi, they would hit social media to thank everyone who gave money or donated used clothes to make this life-changing trip possible, relaying the story of how thrilled the kids were to see them and how they came *running* when the team arrived. Once back home, the missionaries would go on and on about how blessed they were to have so much in the United States while at the same time admiring how joyful poor people were, despite having so little. (Of course, no one ever asks if by giving all those joyful poor people more stuff we're messing with their joy, because it's just too confusing to think about, and it fucks with the tidy narrative. But whatever.) Pleased with the outcome of their mission, they would immediately begin preparations for next year's short-term trip. Everyone knows it can take a while to come up with the $35,000 needed to send fifteen people to Central America to drop off six garbage bags of old clothes and pass out 280 lollipops.

Meanwhile, the Precario would be littered with candy wrappers and, after being shuffled around the community, the clothes nobody wanted could be found covered in dirt and human waste, mixed in with all manner of refuse that lined the sludgy walking paths throughout the shantytown. The kids, many of whom stayed home from school to take full advantage of their gringo visitors, would fall even further behind in their subpar education—taking another tiny step away from any hope of escaping their dire circumstances: an ironic guarantee that in the years to come they'd still be there to teach their own kids how to grin and graciously accept handouts from helpful foreigners. Lord knows they would get plenty of practice. Within a month, another van full of short-term missionaries would come bearing gifts, wide-eyed and well intentioned, and the kids would do it all over again.

To be fair, I'd been struggling with my own presence in the Precario for quite a while. I'd seen how the young men stood and watched us from afar, jaws set firmly and arms crossed. They were *allowing* us to be there, allowing a group of wealthy white women to come into their community because we brought healthy snacks and fun crafts for the kids, but they were not happy to see us and they wanted us to know. I was also struck by how virtually all of the kids' parents disappeared whenever we arrived. Ignoring the fact that with so many unemployed adults living in such close proximity there was never any shortage of child care, I let myself believe everyone took off because they were grateful for an or so hour of free babysitting. But really, would I want to stand there and watch while someone else fed my children? No. I would walk away too. I would let them feed my kid and I'd probably even be grateful, because a free meal is a free meal, but I would not stick around for the show.

The more time I spent in the community, the more I realized that poor people are poor and perhaps un-educated, but they're not dumb. They knew the SUV I drove up in was worth more money than their family would see in twenty years. They knew that my kids went to private schools in Costa Rica and that I lived in a good house on a paved road with a whistle-blowing security guard who patrolled on a bicycle. And while I do think they knew we meant well, I'm pretty sure they also knew we were utterly clueless.

No doubt the paths that lead to poverty in Costa Rica are not unique. The residents of the Precario suffered from alcohol and drug abuse, domestic violence, lack of education and opportunity, government corruption, mental illness, and broken families. But programs that keep poor people fed and clothed often fail to address the problems that keep them poor. In other words? Poverty is hella complicated.

I loved the kids who came to our clubs, and I genuinely wanted to help them, but when I looked out across the expanse of tin and plywood shacks (many of which had DirecTV satellite dishes but no plumbing), it dawned on me that maybe I had no idea what changing their lives would actually require. I could show up every week for a decade to hand out bananas and help toddlers glue cotton balls onto coloring pages with Bible verses, but the complicated lives of the Precario kids would remain just as messy and complex as the first time I'd arrived to "help."

Was I *called* to love and care for the poor? Most definitely.

Was I *equipped* to love and care for Costa Rica's poor in respectful, sensible ways that went to the root of the problem? Like, *not even close.*

As hard as I tried to apply all the feel-good Christian clichés we use as permission to descend on impoverished communities, I couldn't keep pretending that it was actually accomplishing significant change.

———

I used to joke around that when we flew off to the mission field, Steve and I were like the Apostle Paul going blind on the road to Damascus: later the scales would fall from our eyes. I had completely bought into my cause, was fully immersed in the journey with no intention of turning back, only to learn with sudden clarity that I had been *wrong* about so many things on so many levels.

I was blind but now I see.

Now I could see how our uninvited arrival as missionaries was, in itself, patronizing. Now I could see how truly helping people is far more complex, costly, and time-consuming than I'd ever dreamed. Now I could see how well-meaning but ignorant humanitarian aid efforts can actually *hinder* a community's progress. Now I could see how our failure to ask questions and seek answers before we even got on the plane was failing everyone involved.

As the scales fell away, each new revelation left me feeling more foolish, angry, and afraid.

I desperately wanted to do good, but after seeing how easily our best efforts can miss the mark, I found the fear of trying something new and doing it wrong debilitating. I never stopped trusting God and I never felt abandoned by Jesus, but now that I could see? I felt utterly paralyzed by the thought of creating or condoning the next trend in nefarious church bullshit. There was simply no margin left in my weary soul for the catchy clichés, false promises, and overspiritualized expense reports that had played such a pivotal role in my life up to that point. Like a huge doofus, I'd given up everything and turned my children's lives upside down for what I'd finally come to view as a false gospel of Christian missions created to help folks back home feel better.

How could I have ever believed that God was calling me to be a missionary? I was a cranky, cynical, opinionated, depressed, introverted, moody follower of Jesus who, at best, hobbled along on the fringe of the church, unable to get with the program.

What on earth had compelled me to think I could bring anything good to a Central American country already teeming with white weirdos from the North?

17
Natural-Born Blogger

We made a good life in Costa Rica, but every morning I awoke feeling a little more unsure of my place in the world and the church. I would daydream about packing up and going home, but I still felt the gentle prodding of God to look and listen, to stay there and figure shit out. Meanwhile, right under my nose, my whole life was taking a strange and wonderful turn. While Steve, the Very Best Missionary, worked on campus during the week and rolled around in the mud with grown men on weekends, I stayed home in my pajamas with two dogs curled at my feet, and accidentally became a writer.

That might seem super obvious, since you're reading a book that I wrote, so I'm just gonna go ahead and point out that the kind of girl who drops out of high school in the tenth grade isn't usually the same person who daydreams of growing up to write essays on purpose. And I am no exception. I had never done any writing prior to taking responsibility for communicating back home about our missionary life, and I was as surprised as anyone to find that the whole thing came sort of naturally. When thoughts from my brain mixed with feelings from my heart, and then I wrote them down, they came out sounding less, y'know, *stupid*. It's not that I love writing (I don't), but somehow I just *am* a writer.

To be clear, I'm not saying I'm a *good* writer, only that, for whatever reason, I express myself better with my fingers than with my mouth. (*I'm totally judging you, pervert.*)

Blogging as Jamie the Very Worst Missionary (thank you, Mrs. Eatadick) rather than as a representative of my family, my home church, or my sending agency, gave me the freedom to write about anything that struck me as worthy of a few words. I shared silly stories and half-baked thoughts about life and faith, marriage and motherhood, friendship, food, football, and just about everything in between. Sometimes I wrote about the big, important things I was wrestling with, like mental illness and body image and stuff about God. But just as often I wrote about things like the time I accidentally threw a field mouse into the washer with a load of towels. Or how one of the dogs snatched a wild parrot right out of the air and left the most beautiful carnage, a rainbow of bright, sparkly feathers, floating softly around the yard. (Fun fact: The prettier a bird is, the worse I feel when my dog murders it.)

Anyway.

I wrote about our family adventures, like when our car broke down in a Nicaraguan border town and we hitchhiked with our kids to the nearest bus station in the back of a toothless stranger's pickup. And I wrote about things that were less fun, like the time I sat in howler monkey piss on a riverboat, far from home, and hours later I smelled so bad someone drive-by-sprayed me with cheap perfume. And the time a scary dude on the bus asked if I wanted to buy some cocaine and waved his machete in my face. (That's not a penis euphemism—it was an *actual* machete. Good grief, get your mind out of the gutter!) When Steve blew out his knee playing football and had surgery at a nice private hospital in an emerging third-world country, I wrote about it. And when the standard-issue Costa Rican hospital gown wasn't wide enough to cover his butt or long enough to cover his junk, I took a picture. And then I wrote about that too.

The point is, I wasn't posting mind-blowing stuff all over the Internet, but my corner of the Web was gritty and funny and sometimes brutally honest. It was amazing to me when complete strangers showed up to read along and leave comments or shared entries with their friends. (This amazes me still.) Part coffee-shop chat, part confessional, part courtroom, my little public journal soon grew beyond its original audience and original purpose. No subject was off limits, no person beyond reproach, and no process above critique.

Which means that eventually I dove headlong into the complicated feelings I had about missions and missionaries. Admittedly, this was a pretty bold move for someone who was still suckling off the missions tit, so to speak, and it often felt scary and counterintuitive. Nevertheless, I felt I owed it to God and to the church to tell the whole truth.

With an awkward mix of trepidation and defiance, I began pulling back the curtain to give outsiders a better view of short-term mission trips and the long-term missionary lifestyle. To my great relief, the world did not stop spinning. Instead, I heard from loads of people—trusted friends and total strangers around the globe—who were working through similar fears and frustrations with all manner of churchy bullshit.

I was not alone.

I was not the only one sitting in the aftermath, when the carefully crafted Christian facade has collapsed. It was like the air beginning to clear after an explosion, and I was seeing the faces of other stunned survivors stumbling around to find a safe place in a new landscape. Huge numbers of them came forward to express similar misgivings and to ask similar questions about how to love our neighbors and serve our planet in healthier, more productive ways. I wasn't the only one who figured something wasn't right. And for the first time in a long time, I thought maybe I wasn't just being an asshole.

Not everyone agreed with that assessment.

Let me tell you, if one old lady gets super pissed off when you write on your blog that you said "Jesus Shit Balls Christ" after you dropped your drawers to find a gecko creeping right up on Cupid's cupboard, you can imagine what happens if you take to the Internet to ever so gently suggest that perhaps the current state of Christian missions is a billion-dollar Dumpster fire.

It's not pretty.

It turns out, there are actually lots and lots of people who don't like to have their good intentions, perceived sacrifices, and church-sanctioned vacations publicly questioned. I'm dead serious when I say these are generally decent, well-meaning people, but they've been throwing material and human resources into the missions machine without a second thought for as long as they can remember. They don't know what to make of it when you come out of nowhere and tell them they should, *for the love of God, stop.* They are shocked by the sudden news that they might be doing more harm than good to the very people they're trying to help. And they don't like it.

Lord knows a good missionary would have kept her mouth shut about all of it. But I never claimed to be a good missionary, and as the readership of my stupid little blog inexplicably continued to grow, I felt more and more compelled to say these things out loud. It felt like my spiritual duty to speak up.

So I did.

On the blog I started as a wannabe world changer,

I dared to suggest everything about missions is not as awesome and amazing as I had once expected. I mentioned that long-term missionaries sometimes lack a healthy work ethic, sometimes use manipulative language, and sometimes straight up *do not belong* out there. And then I went on to challenge the claims of life-changing greatness made by their short-term cousins.

I asked them to take a long, hard look at the dangerous messages we send to impoverished and marginalized people when we show up on their doorstep to "bless" them with ourselves, our stuff, and our ideas.

I dared do-gooders to look at the big picture. To see how it emasculates a father when we send a bunch of squealing teenage girls with matching T-shirts and brand-new hammers to build a shack for his family over spring break. To consider the impact on small businesses, day laborers, and skilled workers when we show up in their communities to do for free the very job that would have allowed them to put food on their own tables. To acknowledge how orphans are emotionally injured when a never-ending stream of smiling volunteers comes and goes from their lives. And further, to ask if the kids in an orphanage are orphans at all, or if they have been abandoned by struggling families to be raised by a corrupt system that thrives on our ignorance and good intentions.

I defied them to do the math.

In the States, does donating more canned food and collecting more clothes year after year after year speak to the success of serving underresourced communities, or does it indicate a continued failure to help them find their way out of poverty? When Thanksgiving Day is over, and cities across the United States are trashed with *actual tons* of uneaten food and Styrofoam containers, have we made the lives of those who must live in the aftermath of our "service" better? The sewer rats think *yes!* But do the residents? I mean, do they *really*?

Very quickly I learned what happens when you threaten the Christian status quo. People who benefit from "the way it is" (in this case, comfortable suburbanites, long-term missionaries who draw a paycheck off the church, and short-term travelers collecting passport stamps in the name of Jesus) will try to discredit your opinion by devaluing you as a person.

Who are you to judge? they demand to know.

Who was I to complain about the very system that had gotten me into missions in the first place?

Who was I to cast doubt on the people who came before me?

Who was I to wonder about God's intent for the church and for the world?

Who was I to ask such questions? And what they really wanted was for everyone to see that the answer was *Nobody.* That way my opinion was worthless.

To be honest, back in the day—way back in the tender beginning of my journey with Jesus—that bullying tactic might have shut me up. Back then, I might have been content to pull on the missionary mask, adopt the vague spiritual language, and fill a blog with feel-good stories featuring the immeasurable importance of lame euphemisms like "loving on people," "planting seeds," and "being a blessing."

But that time was long over, and that chick was long gone.

When I landed in Costa Rica with my husband, three sons, and a life stripped down enough to be weighed in pounds and ounces, I wasn't a confused little girl anymore. I wasn't a brazen teenager or a needy young wife or a lonely, exhausted mom. I was still broken and wounded, yes, still weak and struggling in so many ways, but in following Jesus, who makes space at the table for everyone, I had discovered my own worth. I was now a woman who knew that despite her brokenness she was intrinsically valuable, not just to God but to the world around her.

I am a woman who's grown confident in the knowledge that her value is not up for review by a flawed and fragile church but already affirmed by the One who knows her best, loves her most, and equipped her over a lifetime to see and to speak up. So when the Internet hordes expressed their displeasure, it truly didn't bother me. When they called me a disgrace, an apostate, a heretic, I genuinely did not care. But I confess that when they tried to make me feel small and insignificant by calling my inherent worth into question, that girl in her badass boots and black leather jacket resurfaced to respond.

Who am I?! I'm so glad you asked. I am the flawed, faithful follower of a radical leader, the lost and found daughter of a good king, an unlikely agent of hope and healing in a hurt world. I am a mother, a sister, a wife, a neighbor, a friend. I am nobody. Just a grown-ass woman with an opinion and a voice. And bitch? I'm pretty sure I was born to call out this bullshit.

If our calling is who we are, not what we do, and our equipping is our practical capacity to serve others, then, based on *who* God created me to be and *how* He equipped me throughout my life, I think maybe I was drawn to Costa Rica for the express purpose of seeing how naïveté and brokenness like my own have affected global missions and humanitarian aid, and then inviting whoever would listen into a difficult but necessary conversation about setting things right.

Isn't it possible that's how God would use a cranky, cynical, opinionated, depressed, introverted, moody follower of Jesus to do a bit of good in a tiny Central American country teeming with white weirdos from the North?

God knew I was *never* going to be a good little missionary. I just don't have it in me. And I think that's exactly why I was there.

18
Practical Magic

If I had to pick one word to describe my journey as a missionary, I would choose "amazing"! Just kidding! I would say it was "confusing."

In two words? "Super confusing."

Three? "Super fucking confusing." You get the idea.

The only thing I can say with any measure of confidence about how things went down in Costa Rica is that it was way too sloppy to be all God's doing and far too miraculous to be all mine. I believe we were both in it, making our own contributions to the story as it unfolded. But I think sometimes it's hard to tell where God's part ends and ours begins, because shit gets kinda squirrelly when the designer of the living universe is all up in your business.

For the longest time I didn't even have language for this thing that happens when your calling meets your equipping and then cool stuff abounds, the way I'd seen with Steve on the football team and then (even more surprisingly) with me on my blog.

I would read awesome viral stories that showed up in my news feed about just the right person doing just the right thing at just the right time, and I'd wonder, *What is that?* Like the eighty-year-old army vet with medic training from the Korean War who just happens to be there to help when he gets stuck, alone, between floors on a hospital elevator with a woman in labor. Or the off-duty firefighter who pulls an unconscious motorist out of a burning car on a deserted country road after a random wrong turn. Or maybe a little group of tenacious punk-ass middle schoolers who see somebody acting suspicious while they're out being obnoxious in their neighborhood, so they call 9-1-1 and end up chasing down a would-be kidnapper on their bicycles.

What are we supposed to call that?

In the world we call it a "coincidence" and in the church we call it "a God thing." But I've begun to think it's more of both, some kind of *practical magic* that happens when your personal capacity comes crashing into God's desire in some unexpected way, at the most unusual time, or in the strangest place. So these days, when I see ordinary people and an extraordinary God working together to make something good happen, that's what I call it—practical magic.

At the very center of this idea is where our stories become truly incredible. When we do what we were designed, equipped, and educated to do best, in the company of a God who continually nudges us in the direction of love, I think that's when we find ourselves in the most productive, most compassionate, most life-changing spaces. Practical magic is why, when we tell our own stories, we can't help but say corny things like "God only knew" and "by the grace of God," even when saying such things seems trite and simplistic.

Looking back across the expanse of my own life, I could easily point to this journey as evidence that miracles happen and God is in control. All I'd have to do is tell the simple but amazing story of a little Jewish kid / rebel youth / teen mom who gave her life to Jesus and became a Christian missionary, and church people would love it. They eat that shit up, for real. But there is another way to look at it, one that paints a fuller but far more complicated picture of how God and I ended up in Costa Rica together, and how it was on purpose but also kind of by accident.

In this version of the story, curiosity and contemplation are part of who I've always been. I was just born this way. Then, as a goofy kid, I was encouraged to ask big, annoying questions and to seek real answers, as the earliest formation of my faith and the base upon which everything else rests was built from bricks of Jewish clay. Out of that introduction to God I carried more than just warm memories of the last night of Hanukkah. I've held on to more than a scant handful of Hebrew words and an abiding love of kosher deli pickles the size of my forearm. Through the practice of those ancient rites and rituals I learned, very young, that God loves and expects our questions, and though I stopped practicing ages ago, I never stopped asking.

Later, while I was an insecure teenage girl hiding behind a tough front, I accidentally grew a thick skin. Ew, not, like, *literally*. I mean the figurative kind of thick skin that helps a person receive criticism, handle opposition, and even stand up under verbal attack. It's a "fake it till you make it" kinda thing, and I'd gotten so good at pretending I didn't care what other people thought of me that eventually I started to believe it. When I was young, this exterior confidence was merely a facade, but as a grown woman and follower of Jesus, that toughness found a healthy spot to settle in my soul. Throughout my life, the ability to switch off the part of my brain that might otherwise long for the approval of strangers has been a gift.

Even depression, my relentless companion, will get its name in the end credits of this story for creating a gaping hole in my life—a barren, blank space that I would unexpectedly learn to fill with words.

So while it's true that on the surface I was probably the most unlikely candidate in history to become a Christian missionary, that's not the cool part of the story. The cool part is that if God was angling to change a broken system and wanted to spark conversations and ask hard questions (knowing that some people would come back swinging), on a purely practical level, I came highly qualified for the job.

Is it obvious or extraordinary? I'm convinced the answer is both. Our lives unfold in ways that are both plain *and* mysterious, because God's equipping is *practical*, but His redemption is *magical*.

The thing is, to be practical is to be accountable. It requires that we embrace the most sensible means of service to others and forces us to evaluate our work based on real results and to determine our success based on actual outcomes, rather than on personal intent. The practical way is not ambiguous, it's not mysterious, it's not romantic. And no matter how well trained and prepared we are, a practical approach to making the world a better place (whether for one person or for one million) is still no guarantee that we will achieve what we hope.

Practical magic asks us to admit when we fail, to cease what is harmful, and to fix what is broken, because what's practical implores us to do better—but what's magical frees us to keep trying. That God *can* redeem our garbage does not justify our churning out the same mindless crap over and over. The magic of redemption invites us to try something new. And in this we don't need to feel ashamed or humiliated by what we didn't get right the first time, for in His desire to heal the world, God wastes nothing.

Not even the very worst thing.

In Costa Rica I also learned that if you want to love someone well, occasionally it really is as simple as "see a need, fill a need." This was true for me on a dark and stormy night when a hungry stranger came knocking at my door.

Squeaking, actually. He was *squeaking* at the door.

I could barely hear it over the high winds and heavy rains, but I'm kind of sensitive to stupid, annoying background noise. When I yelled at my kids to "shut off that god-awful game before I throw it out the window," they said they weren't playing games, so I went on a rampage to find the culprit. I finally figured out that the nonstop *squeak squeak squeak* was coming from right outside the front door. This was a little bit alarming, because the front door was about fifteen feet from the front gate, which I knew for a fact was locked, so the squeaker, whoever it was, must have either broken the deadbolt or squeezed through the bars. Neither of those prospects made me want to open the door, but that awful squeaking was making me wanna punch babies, and I had to make it stop.

As soon as I unlatched the door, the wind pushed it open and an emaciated kitten, no more than a month old, looked up at me. It had appeared out of nowhere in search of food, shelter, and a sucker to con.

Well, it had found the perfect mark. I was obviously a lady who spent a great deal of time in her pajamas and who could appreciate a discerning feline's taste for high-priced cat food with words like "meaty filets" and "rich gravy" on the label. All the kitten had to do was meow through the gap under the front door eleven thousand times, and when it finally opened, there was Sugar Mama, bathed in light from above, like an angel with a soft, doughy lap just waiting for the right kitty to come along and sweep her onto her big fat ass.

Why, hello there.

That tiny wet blob of black fur looked up at me with eyes that were way too big for its head, then marched inside without waiting for an invitation. Of course I rushed to offer our little guest a plate of rice and beans, because that's just what I did, and while it attacked its food, I looked it over carefully. The scrawny fluff ball (a) did not appear to be injured and (b) did appear to be a girl.

Here was a random stray cat dropped on our doorstep by a tropical storm (probably sent to us by the Devil in a bolt of lightning), and I had a suspicion that Steve would not be on board with keeping it, but Steve wasn't home, was he? So there was no one around to stop us when the kids and I fell madly in love and named our new little buddy Knives.

The name started as an homage to the girlfriend, Knives Chau, in *Scott Pilgrim vs. the World*, which we were watching for the seventy-fifth time that evening. And when *the claws* made their first appearance, slicing through the air like Wolverine, we knew we had chosen correctly.

For the record, I swear I told the boys we could keep the kitten only until the animal shelter opened on Monday, and *I really meant it*. But I'd never dealt with cat sorcery before, so I had no idea that keeping a kitten for a weekend and then dropping it off at a shelter is actually *an impossible thing to do*. Like, it cannot be done by mere mortals.

Needless to say, on Monday we became Knives's

forever family, and a few weeks later "she" grew balls and we had to switch pronouns. Mr. Knives Chow Wright has been tripping me on the stairs, attacking my feet from under the bed, spying on me from around corners, slashing at my hands, kneading my belly fat like bread dough, staring at me without blinking, and planning my ultimate demise ever since. He quickly established his lordship over the dogs, who, though much larger and more physically powerful, learned to obediently make way for His Highness, the cat.

I don't mean to brag, but Knives is a hellion if ever one lived, and when he was a stranger, I welcomed him. When he was hungry, I gave him something to eat. When he was thirsty, I gave him something to drink. I'd be hard-pressed to claim his arrival on my doorstep that night was God's idea, but I will say that when I met his basic needs by the most practical means, it changed both of our lives in tangible ways (he eats more; I bleed more), and I suppose that makes Knives my greatest success.

In the spirit of practical magic, I trust that God can redeem even this. Five years as a missionary, and the only thing I really saved was an asshole cat.

———

One day I came downstairs to find Knives curled up in the centerpiece on the dining room table. He had made himself comfortable by scattering its contents all over the place—that way he could use the wooden tray as a chaise longue. The tray had been filled with coarse sand, pebbles, and sea glass—now strewn across table, chairs, and floor. It was the kind of mess I normally would have swept up and thrown away. But this was no ordinary stuff. Every particle of it had come to Costa Rica in a gallon-sized ziplock bag, given a place in our limited luggage space like rare gems.

Originally the makings of that centerpiece came from a beach in northern California, where the city used to dump everybody's garbage right into the water. Like, they would just back the garbage trucks up to the bluff and launch their shit into the sea. Household trash, old dishes, busted jars and bottles, broken appliances, logging refuse, old cars—it all went over the cliffs. Eventually someone realized this was a terrible idea, so they stopped, but by then the area was so polluted it had to be temporarily closed as a public safety hazard.

Nearly fifty years later, Steve and I hiked down to that same beach at low tide, carefully picking our way past fly-swarmed piles of rotting kelp, smelly deposits of dead fish, empty beer cans, and layers of mucky brown foam. It was still super gross, and everything about the trip toward the water screamed, *Dump! You're walking in a garbage dump—for funzies!* The smell alone made me wonder if the sand filling my shoes was toxic enough to kill me, but we'd heard rumors that it would be worth it, so we trudged on. By the time we got to the water's edge, and the sun glistened and danced across the wet surface of the rocks, I had to agree they were right. It was worth it.

It was a remarkable sight—a whole entire beach covered in bits of tumbled glass.

Green and brown and red, with bright blues and bits of turquoise nestled among the cloudy white beads, all of it roughed down and rounded off like smooth stones from so many years of rolling along in the surf. It was stunning—one of those crazy, beautiful moments in life that catches you off guard and takes your breath away, because you never, ever expected garbage to be so . . . I don't know . . . *perfect.* We stayed for hours, looking for treats in what used to be trash, amazed at how the sea could turn a community disaster around and serve up a national treasure.

It was practically magical.

Since that day, I've kept a trayful of Glass Beach on the dining room table as a centerpiece of sorts. What started as a few handfuls of rocks and sand that Steve and I scooped up and brought home in an empty McDonald's bag became a monument to our loved ones over the years. All of our best and dearest people have sat with us around the sea glass at one time or another—sorting it, swirling it, searching through it with distracted fingertips, looking for the right words to talk about life. That little pile of rocks has been privy to incredible stories and agonizing secrets. I would swear those bits of tumbled glass have some sort of therapeutic quality, except I know they don't. The truth is it's not the rocks that have drawn us back to the table to share. It's an altogether different centerpiece that calls us to sit with one another and talk awhile.

The first time I stood on Glass Beach, I remember thinking, *This is what God does!*

God takes our crap offerings, our messed-up lives, *our garbage*, and turns it around on us. He makes it beautiful somehow. Against all odds, God redeems what seems hopelessly trashed and broken and refashions it into something different. And somewhere along the line, this God who will make all things new had become the centerpiece of our lives. So I brought my ziplock bag of Glass Beach all the way to Costa Rica to serve as a reminder.

This is practical magic.

It was around this very centerpiece that we were sitting after dinner one night with some of our favorite football players, Tomás and Eduardo, and Ed's smart, gorgeous fiancée, Juliana, when she smiled and said, *"Hay algo que tengo que decirles."* There's something I have to tell you.

She explained that after our many talks about life and faith and Jesus, she and Ed had decided to go to church. In fact, they'd been attending a church near her house for a few months, she said, and it had changed her life. Juli and Ed told us it was in part because of our honesty regarding the messiness of church that they were able to walk in with fresh eyes and realistic expectations, unafraid to ask questions or offer their opinions. They'd found a community they loved and felt part of, and there they'd met Jesus. But the reason she was bringing it up was that she was planning on being baptized by her pastor and they hoped we could be there for the special occasion.

On a bright tropical morning just a few weeks later, we prayed for Juli and cheered with joy as, surrounded by her family and friends, her local pastor dunked her for Jesus.

Three days later, we left Costa Rica for good.

We spent our last Sunday in the country the same way we'd spent our first, at a swimming-pool baptism, celebrating one person's hope-filled commitment to a lifetime of giving and receiving unconditional love. And it was the same, but *so different*.

I mean, talk about coming full circle—to end like that, the way we began.

It was like God wanted us to see how much we'd learned and changed and grown throughout those tumultuous years abroad. It was a painful reminder of how arrogant and naive and stupid we had been when we arrived—jumping in like we had any right—and it was a grace-filled affirmation that it was time for us to go.

In the end, we were simply too practical to stay, and God was too magical to let us.

19

Stuck with Knives

The decision to move back to the United States did not come to us quickly or easily.

With the end of our five-year commitment looming, Steve and I spent approximately three and a half million hours talking, praying, and searching for the best way forward. We were begging God to show us what to do, and with each passing day, it became more and more apparent that we could not continue to live as missionaries with any sense of conviction. That's not to say we thought it was all for nothing, only that the line between the good and the bad had grown too blurry.

There was a healthy way for us to stay in Costa Rica, if that's what we wanted, but we agreed that the only responsible way to remain would be to find "real jobs," pay our own way, and fully integrate like normal immigrants or expats. We believed that if we stayed it would be time to love our neighbors and invest in the community apart from both the agenda and the safety net of the North American church—and free from the relational guillotine of the title "missionary." Steve was getting paid to coach football, but when we crunched the numbers, we decided our family probably couldn't make it work on his stipend of 17,000 colones (about thirty-five dollars) a week.

The thought of saying good-bye to our players and the rest of the football community was truly gut-wrenching. There was so much love and life and, like, *spirit-filled Jesus juju* surrounding the team, if we could have found *any* way to reconcile our hearts with staying on as missionaries, I think we would have. It would have been a relatively easy transition too, since all I'd have had to do was write one blog post about how we felt "called to redirect our energy to sports ministry," and boom, it would be done. I have no doubt that most, if not all, of our incredibly kind and generous supporters would have continued to give to our work. I also have no doubt that, had we stayed, God would have done what God always does and made it worthwhile for somebody. But that wasn't reason enough.

During our last year in Costa Rica, amid mounting frustration, Steve and I continued to grow passionate about calling attention to the problems that plague Christian missions. We felt inspired to explore new and better ways for flawed followers of Jesus to engage the world, to love their neighbors, and to make an actual difference in the lives of people around them. I could continue to write on the subject from wherever we lived, but neither of us could do much to instigate change directly from the mission field, especially while we were still dependent on the system financially.

After months of scouring Internet job postings, our home church offered Steve a role as the director of outreach and missions, and it seemed like a golden opportunity to take everything we'd gained from our experiences and pay it forward. To be able to share the painful lessons we'd learned with a community of people we already knew well and loved dearly felt like a gift. If we couldn't change missions from the mission field, we thought, why not try to do it from within the church? Steve accepted the position, and I booked our family on a one-way flight that would take us back to California a week shy of our fifth anniversary in Costa Rica.

———

Sometimes I think my whole life could be summed up by a long list of things I never wanted to see, or do . . . or eat. (Chicken feet come to mind.) Well, at four o'clock in the morning on July 11, 2012, I added "Carry an angry black cat through airport security with bare hands" to that ever-expanding file.

For the second time in our lives, we sold, tossed, and donated nearly all of our material possessions, packed the precious remainder in ten familiar duffel bags, five carry-ons, and four backpacks, and set off to start over in a faraway land. But this time things would be different. This time our kids knew exactly where they were going. This time we spoke the language and knew the culture. This time, when we pulled up to the departures curb in front of the airport for an international move, our baggage would include a ten-foot surfboard (which hasn't seen water since and probably never will again), two rescue dogs, and the Devil's cat.

Since they weren't service dogs (apparently eating used toilet paper out of the trash isn't *technically* considered a service), Osita and Gringa had to be crated and flown as cargo. At the check-in desk I showed all the necessary paperwork, paid transportation fees, and gave each dog a good scruffle behind the ears before nervously handing them over to the airline. They started to bark and whine as they were wheeled away on rolling carts, but I could hear the baggage handlers crooning back gently and making little kissy noises to calm them, so it seemed like they were in good hands. With a sigh of relief, I turned to join my boys in the growing line that snaked its way through the gamut of airport security. I was about to find out, the hard way, that getting the cat on the plane would *not* be so easy.

Poor Knives was not at all happy about this move to the United States, and I could hardly blame him. Costa Rica was the only home he'd ever known, the only place he'd stalked geckos, terrorized small birds, and collected the dead bodies of rodents to show off like he'd actually won them out of a claw machine. He knew nothing of the world but hunting in coffee fields, dominating packs of stray dogs, and scrambling in out of the rain. But leaving him behind was not an option—he was stuck with us, and we were stuck with him.

Knives was curled up in the cat carrier as we approached the airport metal detector, and everything would have been fine if he'd been allowed to stay that way. I set him down, walked through the scanner, and reached back to take the carrier from a security guard who held it out toward me. But she didn't hand Knives over. Instead, she instructed me to remove him from his cage and walk him through the metal detector in my arms. I looked at her in sheer horror like *You know this is a* terrible *plan, right? Have you seen* The Silence of the Lambs?

But she insisted. So against my better judgment I opened the cage door, stuck in a sacrificial arm, and brought forth nine pounds of biting, clawing, moaning, hissing, tail-whipping psychopath.

Knives is not the kind of cat you hold, or even really touch, when he doesn't want you to. But I knew there would be absolute carnage if I lost control of that animal in an airport packed with vacationing families, dirty hippies, and drug dealers. Fortunately, he seemed to be pretty certain that I alone was to blame for this disruption of his comfort, so he sank his teeth into my hand, wrapped his body around my arm like a boa constrictor, and went to work on my flesh with those mutant claws.

And I let him. Because I'm pretty much a hero.

Once everyone was satisfied that Knives wasn't concealing a belt buckle, bobby pins, or a loaded revolver in his fur, I went to pry him off my bloody stump and return him to the safety of his carrier. But the agent stopped me again and waved her explosive-sniffing wand to point us toward the next station of the exam.

"I have to swab the cat," she said with great authority, as if she catches cat bombers, like, *all the time*. I don't know why, but on our way over to the desk, I started to plead Knives's case, saying, "He looks kinda shady, but I can honestly say I've never seen this cat make a bomb. Not even once!" And then I remembered who we were dealing with, and how at that very moment he was skinning me alive, and I was like, "Okay. Yeah. Probably better to check."

Sweaty and bloody, I did eventually make it onto an airplane, along with Steve, our three incredible sons (all teenagers now), two dogs in the pressurized cargo hold, one *very* unhappy cat under the seat in front of me, and the shredded remnants of my pride. Thanks to Knives, my arm looked exactly how my spirit felt.

Just as our plane lifted off, the sun came up over the horizon, and a heart-sized lump leaped into my throat. With tears threatening to spill, I pulled out my phone and snapped one last picture of the emerald-green country my family had called home for five years. Was I disappointed? Grateful? Relieved? Happy? Heartbroken? I didn't know how to feel as we climbed into the sky, but I couldn't stop thinking about all the things I wished I had done differently, the stuff I wished I'd known sooner, and the people I wished I'd loved better while we were still there.

But it was done. All I could do was watch through a little oval window as Costa Rica and my missionary life disappeared behind me.

———

Just like that, we moved back to our little beige house on the same beige street in a boring beige suburb, and Steve started work at a great big beige church.

On Steve's first day in the office, the boys were out catching up with their grandparents, so I poured myself a cup of coffee and sat down alone on the floor in the middle of a house with no furniture (just a coffee-maker, because *priorities*), and the space felt empty and still and uncomfortably quiet. No noise filtered in from the street. There were no roosters crowing, no dogs barking, no shouting salesmen, not even the racket of a security guard on a bicycle chasing a couple of loose cows out of the neighborhood with his trusty whistle. There was just . . . nothing. I sat there for the longest time in the weird suburban silence, wondering, *What the hell am I supposed to do next?* The problem was that I was completely overwhelmed by both the felt needs of the world and the brokenness of the church, and I didn't know where to start, or what to do, or how to really help.

Just as I was about to get up off the cold bare floor,

Knives strolled over and curled up in the warm nest of my crisscrossed legs. (He has a gift for knowing exactly when I'm about to get up and deciding that is when he wants to be petted.) I was now effectively trapped, unable to leave that spot, because once a cat is on top of any part of your body, some kind of kitty mind control forces you to stay put until they're done napping. I can't explain it. I just knew I was gonna be there for a while, stuck with Knives. Which was actually kinda fitting, because I had *just* been telling God how on the heels of this big move back to California, which should have built momentum into my life, I felt more stuck than ever.

During my feline-enforced #quiettime, I kept coming back to a piece of advice I'd been given by several friends. It's just one of those things you say to someone when you're trying to be encouraging, but I'd heard it so many times, thinking about it made me want to jump up and run into traffic. (Thank God the cat was holding me down.)

Do the next right thing. That was their advice.

Seriously?

DO THE NEXT RIGHT THING?

Well, fuck me in both ears. Why didn't anybody tell me all I had to do this whole time was "the next right thing"!

How blissfully simple.

I think most of us would love to do the next right thing, but what if, like me, you feel overwhelmed and paralyzed because you don't know what the next right thing is? What if your life is actually super complicated, and you have lots of experience doing what you thought was the right thing only to have it end up being totally wrong?

I mean, maybe it would be more helpful if "the next right thing" was more specific, like "*Eat* the next right thing" or "Do the next right *yoga pose*." But my life is more like choosing which direction to go at a fork in the road to Oz and less like picking breakfast off a Cracker Barrel menu. For the things that really matter, I'm gonna need a better slogan.

Forgive me, but I'd like a catchphrase that captures both the responsibility I feel to do good and the freedom I have to get it wrong. Because when I'm feeling stuck, which is kind of a lot, it's usually because I'm paralyzed by fear of doing the next *wrong* thing. That morning, stuck to the floor by my rotten cat, I didn't need a cute little meme to cheer me up and let me off the hook. I needed someone to tell me, "Do the next most practical thing after careful exploration of the facts, so that even if it turns out to be the wrong thing, at least you can say you made a solid decision based on sound research, and if after a period of evaluation you find out it wasn't the right thing, then you can try something else. God will handle the rest."

It won't fit on a cross-stitch, but at least we can all sleep at night if things go south.

I will always be grateful for the experiences my family had overseas, and I can honestly say that most days I'm glad we went for it. The truth is, I feel pretty lucky to have lived the life I've lived, to have made the mistakes I've made, and to have seen the hard truths I've seen. Even the part where I earnestly tried to follow God to a faraway land to save the world but found myself in a club full of goobers and dickheads with a gecko in my pants was *pretty amazing*.

Costa Rica sent me home with a cat, two dogs, and a finely tuned crap detector. With keener vision, I've become more and more uncomfortable with exporting the lily-white Jesus of the North American church and even more convinced that God and the world deserve far better than what we've been throwing at them for decades. To be a complicit partner in a billion-dollar industry, to continue to show up, as we so often do, unprepared and ill equipped, to keep sending the wrong people to the wrong places to do the wrong things? This is not an option.

But neither is hiding at home.

To be perfectly honest, a huge part of me wanted to stay right there, safely stuck to the floor with Knives for the rest of my life; a disgruntled ex-missionary, permanently immobilized by the cat in her lap and the fear of becoming next year's embarrassing Christian anecdote.

But that morning, while Knives snoozed, I realized there was actually something I could do and do well. In fact, I was already doing it. I had considered shutting down TheVeryWorstMissionary.com since technically I wasn't one anymore, but I resolved to keep it alive and to continue to write about my eye-opening experiences abroad. I would do *the next practical thing*—and leave it up to God to forge a future and purpose beyond my wildest dreams.

I couldn't know it then, but in the months ahead I would become an advocate for better mission practices worldwide, a journalist for humanitarian aid efforts, and a proponent of education and economic development in impoverished communities. Over the next few years, tapping into my truest self and doing what I do best would take me all over the world, opening doors I never imagined I'd have the opportunity to walk through.

But first, in order to move forward, I would have to look back and let go of the shame I carried from my own mistakes and missteps. I would have to trust our years in Costa Rica to God (who thus far hadn't let me down), choosing to believe He wouldn't allow even my worst best attempt to save the world to go to waste.

I would simply pursue the most practical ways to love my neighbor, care for creation, and, yes, make the world a better place. I wanted to do something with the knowledge I'd gained, so I decided to gather my courage, cling to the messy meme of practical magic, and rise to *try again.*

I mean . . . just as soon as Knives woke up.

20

Do Your Best

In the beginning this was a story about how *not* to save the world, and it still is. I still have no idea how to fix a big, broken church. I still don't know how to end global poverty. I still haven't come up with a surefire way to heal the emotional, physical, and spiritual wounds of an entire planet full of diverse and dynamic people. Like, I have *no idea* how to do any of those things. (And to be fair, you probably should have clued in on that about, oh, I don't know, like fifteen chapters ago? So that's kind of on you.)

Don't get me wrong, I have *tons* of ideas about how to improve Christian missions (most involve gasoline and a match), but the last thing anybody needs is another one-size-fits-all prescription for charging out into the world in the name of Jesus.

I am certain of only two things. The first is that when Jesus told me to love my neighbor, I'm pretty sure he meant, like, my *actual neighbor*—the person or people nearest to me at any given moment. At home. At work. On the subway. In the supermarket. On a street corner. Y'know, *neighbors*. And the second thing is this: The only way to know how to truly *love* your neighbor is to truly *know* your neighbor.

And that's it. That is the single concrete conclusion I gathered from five years as a paid professional neighbor lover. *You're welcome.*

The point is, I can't tell you how to change your piece of the world, because I've probably never even met your neighbors. Obviously, they know what they need, so I would tell you to go ask them. Though I do wonder if maybe there aren't still some questions you need to ask yourself before you go barging into unknown territory with your sword of righteousness aloft.

Anyway. Instead of a comprehensive how-to list, I'd like to offer you what I hope will be a little word of encouragement.

Relax. This isn't gonna be weird. I have no intention of congratulating you for being made of stardust and unicorn farts. But I do want to leave you with something to come back to, should you ever find yourself buried in the avalanche of your own evolving faith.

—

While coming "home" provided relief from the daily frustrations of life in a second language and another culture, I stumbled out of the mission field into the waiting arms of the North American church. From missionary to pastor's wife. *Frying pan, meet fire.*

I found it was one thing to ask questions and even to have doubts from behind a computer screen, but the same people who had seemed anxious to dismiss my questions from afar tried to scold me for my observations in person. They liked to say things like "Tearing things down is easy" and "Complaints should come with solutions." And at first this shut me up. But the thing is, you don't have to have solutions prepared before you point out legitimate problems. That's bullshit and it doesn't even make sense.

Think about it. If someone pointed out that you had a rash, you wouldn't refuse to look at it if they couldn't also tell you how to treat it. That would be the dumbest thing ever. If I told my husband I could hear that something was wrong with our car, he wouldn't say, "Talk to me when you know how to fix it." You don't have to understand how to cure someone to know and care that they are sick. When it comes to making the world a better place, we should all be looking for helpful ways forward, so don't let anyone convince you that you shouldn't engage in hard conversations. Your voice matters.

And listen. People who believe that "tearing things down is easy" have clearly never done it. At least not properly. So they don't understand that tearing down the early versions of your own faith (even that annoying chick with the mom bob and the gold cross) is like taking a sledgehammer to your childhood home. It's not easy to dismantle the very things that helped make you who you are. It's not easy to stay grateful for your own journey while you acknowledge that certain parts of it were incredibly unhealthy and shouldn't be perpetuated.

But while tearing down things you once loved to make room for something new is never easy (it's super fucking hard), harder still is figuring out what "something new" is supposed to look like and then learning how to build it from the ground up. This is especially daunting when you're still in the middle of clearing off your spiritual foundation and picking through the debris.

For me, the experience of dismantling my simple ideology felt bittersweet. It was necessary and liberating, and at times it felt damn good, but it was also sad, and confusing, and lonely. It's *scary* to get back up after you've been crushed by the realization that the church you grew up in or the ministry you championed or the spiritual leaders you adored, supported, and trusted were perhaps not as *awesome* and *amazing* as you once believed. If they turn out to be abusers, liars, crooks, pathological narcissists, and/or asshats in general, it's worse, and some people never recover from the pain, anger, and disappointment.

I read something somewhere (like, in the Bible maybe?), about a bunch of religious leaders who were screaming at Jesus about shit like upholding the law and honoring traditions and doing things the way they'd always been done. It was a Sabbath day, and when they challenged him about working on a holy day of rest, Jesus went right out and found a man who'd been living on the fringe for far too long, deemed by the religious to be unclean and unwelcome because of a shriveled arm. Jesus approached the man and said, "Stretch out your hand." When he did, his arm was fully restored. And for doing the work of healing on the Sabbath, Jesus was accused of breaking the laws. The leadership went bonkers, and self-righteous freaking out ensued.

I point out that story because what we're talking about isn't new. The world has long been full of hurt and need, but religious leaders are often too tightly bound to their own agenda to offer any real help. It's been like this for ages. But Jesus isn't interested in preserving the way it's always been. He came to heal the paralyzed, so you don't have to stay *stuck*.

Jesus heals the sick, the blind, the lame, and the broken, and that includes battered souls and fractured hearts and brains that have forgotten how to think for themselves. Many of us have been hurt by the church, but to be redeemed by God is to understand that, though you have been wounded, you don't have to keep bleeding. You are redeemed. Now you can *see*. Now you can *stand*. To trust God is to *stretch out your hand*.

To bring light and hope, you and I must show up for life in our homes, in our neighborhoods, in our workplaces, and in our schools not as "missionaries" and self-proclaimed blessings but as imperfect parents, genuine friends, competent professionals, and messy people. We must show up as safe havens, not as mini saviors. We must bravely show up in our everyday lives to do our best with what we have, listening carefully, serving sensibly, and loving fully as active participants in the story of who God is and what God does.

If you have a pulse—regardless of your age, race, nationality, gender, religion, or politics—you are probably already working in collaboration with the creator of the universe to write the story of the planet Earth. That's why you're so damn tired!

How we speak to a waiter, treat a beggar, spend a dollar—with every action we take, we are creating the world we live in. We get to decide whether our contribution to this story is patience or exasperation, compassion or condemnation, awareness or foolishness, liberation or enslavement. We can't go back and erase the parts we're not proud of, but we can move forward different and better.

We don't need to spend another second of our life wondering about our spiritual calling, because we're already right here in the thick of it. We're already called. It doesn't matter where you live, whom you know, what you can do, or how much you have to offer; you were called into the fray on the day you were born, and your calling is *love*.

Love God and love others. That's the whole deal.

But to love others well, we have to see them as whole people in a big picture, not just as cute little vignettes to be used in our own narrative. We have to remember that no matter how rich, poor, foreign, different, or messed up they might seem, they are as called by God and as rich in love as we are. For me, that meant seeing that Costa Rican football players, Nicaraguan coffee pickers, wealthy expats, poor Precario moms, and even all those dumb-ass missionaries whose paths crisscrossed my own were also writers of the story—and that, like me, they were probably doing their best.

Sometimes our story lines will come together, and we'll get to create something inspiring and uplifting, hopefully something that honors God and people. But conflict and tension are unavoidable. They're just what happens when there are this many characters with different motivations and we all bring our own ideas about what should come next.

So, as much as it depends on you and me, let's agree to write an epic of love to the benefit of others.

I can't say exactly what this is all supposed to look like for you—our roles in God's wild purpose for the world are as unique as each of us. But I imagine that our mission of mercy is similar, and it might look a little like this:

> Show up as needed to love your neighbor with your eyes wide open and your arms outstretched. Start by doing your best . . . and then, tomorrow, do better.

On my fortieth birthday, I stretched out my arm and got a big fat tattoo. It goes from shoulder to elbow, in full color, super traditional Americana style, and it has, like, a swallow in flight over a heart above an anchor, and there's some rope and flowers and stuff, and the swallow is holding a banner that says "Act Justly, Love Mercy, Walk Humbly." Okay, okay, I'm sorry! *I know!* The only thing worse than listening to someone describe their tattoo is listening to them explain the dream they had the other night. I apologize if I sound like a huge douche right now, and I promise I'm not trying to be annoying. But I think the tattoo itself is relevant here, because right after I got it, I felt a little twinge of *oh-my-god-what-have-I-done.*

Don't get me wrong, I still love this tattoo, I still think it's beautiful, and I passionately stand behind the Bible verse that inspired it (Micah 6:8, if you care). But one of the things you learn within the first week after getting a tattoo that people can see when you're fully dressed is that you're going to get the same ten questions and comments from complete strangers (mostly dude bros in tank tops) every summer day for the rest of your life:

> "Did that hurt?"
> "Nice ink."
> "How long did that take?"
> "I like your ink."
> "I don't like tattoos."

"I don't like tattoos on girls."

"I *looove* girls with tattoos."

"Who did your ink?"

"Can I see the whole thing?"

"What does it say?"

"Do you have any other ink?"

A visible tattoo may as well be a neon sign that says, "Come talk to me!" which is reason enough for me as an introvert to wish I'd gone with a less visible placement. But the real problem is that to wear these words on my flesh is the equivalent of having one of those Christian fish thingies on my car, *except worse*, because if someone sees me do something shitty, I can't just lie and say I wasn't the one driving. My flesh and my soul are now accountable to each other—permanently, visually, and publicly. I can make excuses for my behavior a thousand ways to Sunday, but if at the end of the day I fail to act with justice, mercy, and humility, I have to own that. And *everybody* knows it.

But actually nothing has changed.

I was already accountable to God and others for the way I live. It's just that this tattoo put me face to face with some of my own gross hypocrisy. If I look in the bathroom mirror and I'm wearing a T-shirt that was made by slave labor over the words "Act Justly," I have to answer for that.

When I catch my reflection in a store window as I'm actively trying to avoid making eye contact with a mentally ill homeless guy who's waving to catch the attention of the chick with "Love Mercy" written on her arm, I have to answer for that.

When I see myself through the eyes of my family, friends, and neighbors, looking more like a powder keg full of outrage, impatience, and irritability, angry enough to punch puppies, I have to answer to the words "Walk Humbly" printed clearly across my very own bicep.

And I have to answer not *later*, when I'm dead, but *now*. Right now. Today. Because every time I look in the mirror, the story I'm writing with my life is staring straight back at me.

About a month after I got this tattoo, a super old man came up to me in a hardware store and asked if he could see it. I pulled my sleeve up over my shoulder to give him a view of the whole thing, which he took a very long time to examine. I never know what to do or what to say when this happens. It's like figuring out what to do with your hands when someone is taking your picture. In these tattoo-inspection situations, I just don't know how long I'm supposed to stand still or which way to turn my head. It usually feels like I cut the person off too early or pull my sleeve down too late. It's awkward. Anyway.

Looking it over, the old man gave a little whistle of approval, and then he read it out loud: "Act justly. . . . Love mercy. . . . Walk humbly."

I said, "Yup. That's what it says."

And then he looked at me and asked, "So *do* you?"

I was like, "Do I what?"

He said, "Do you act justly, love mercy, and walk humbly?"

No one had ever asked me that, and it caught me completely off guard. I stammered, "Oh . . . um, no. No, I guess not. . . . I mean, not really. Not *always*. . . . But *I want to*. I really do."

Then he gave me a wink and warm, wise smile, and with a fatherly pat on the arm, he said, "I'll keep trying if you will."

I nodded and smiled back.

"I'll do my best."

ACKNOWLEDGMENTS

First, and most important, thank you to my sons, Stephen, Dylan, and Jamison, who never need to read this book, because they had to live it. Some will wonder why you three don't feature more prominently in these pages and the truth is, I thought a lot about how and when to include you. But I imagine that your perspective as children who were dragged across the world by your rather unstable parents is a little different from mine. I simply couldn't do justice to the heartache, fear, and loneliness inflicted upon you as kids, and it wasn't fair to leave that part out of the story. Neither could I accurately capture the courage, willingness, and enduring humor you brought to our adventures. In the end, I realized that's a whole other book and, quite frankly, it's not mine to write. Good or bad, we gave you your childhood, and that means you own it. It's yours. So, in general, I left you—my three favorite and most beloved people—out of my first memoir, not as an act of exclusion, but in an attempt to honor you. Should you ever decide to tell your story in your words, you have my blessing (even if I look like a dipshit). Thank you for letting me be your mom, for loving me despite my messiness, and for still speaking to me now that you're all grown up and totally don't have to. You are the absolute best!

There aren't enough words to convey my thankfulness for Steve, who built me a lovely office, handed me the keys, and said, "Now go write." You trusted me to tell our story even when it wasn't favorable, and that's a pretty big deal. I am beyond grateful for everything you've ever done for me.

If not for a brave circle of spiritual sisters, this book would never have happened. You girls amaze and inspire me, you teach me, you love me, and you make me laugh until I pee. You told me I could write a book, and I trust you so much, I had no choice but to believe you. You are a fierce bunch of kick-ass women, and I'm honored to be counted among you. #ASSSForever

My brother, Scott, and sister-in-law, Sarah, saw me through every tiny detail of this long process with interest and enthusiasm. Plus, playdates with Georgia and Penny were my greatest and most consistent respite from writing, I honestly would have died without them. Thank you for everything!

To my clever sisters, Sarah and Emily, my wonder twin, the *other* Jaime, my brilliant cheerleader, Libby, and the greatest mom-in-law of all time, Patty, who saved my sanity by calling, texting, and dragging me out of my office for coffee dates, lunch breaks, and long late-night chats—I owe you each a cheesecake and a million dollars. Thanks for not quitting me.

My friends in SFB, to whom I am so grateful for allowing me to share in their collective humor, outrage, kindness, honesty, intelligence, and general badassery—thank you. Everyone should be so lucky.

Sincere thanks also to: My literary agent, Rachelle Gardner, who waited six long years for my proposal and never stopped gently reminding me. The whole team at Convergent Books, but especially David Kopp, who guided me through the scary world of book writing with the patience of a saint, and didn't make me feel like The Very Worst Author (even though I blew a hundred deadlines and used *tons of italics* and ALL CAPS, and also, about, a dozen, commas in, pretty much, every, sentence). And my hero editor, Heather Kopp, who literally saved my shitty first draft from the trash heap and helped mold it into a thing that I'm not completely embarrassed to let people see.

Last, I offer my heartfelt gratitude to the original readers, you who stumbled across an ugly amateur blog so many years ago and kept coming back for more. You were the first to call me a *writer,* and your encouragement changed my life. When my laptop died, you came together (before crowdsourcing was even a thing) and surprised me with a new MacBook—hand delivered to Costa Rica—so that I wouldn't stop writing. That was the greatest vote of confidence I'd ever received, and it came from a bunch of strangers. How do you thank people you've never met for giving you the gift of purpose? I mean, at the very least, I probably owe you guys a beer or something.

Cheers!

ABOUT THE AUTHOR

JAMIE WRIGHT is a writer and speaker best known for her snarky faith and lifestyle blog, *The Very Worst Missionary*. As a passionate advocate for missions reform and humanitarian aid that is sensible, meaningful, and enduring, she has traveled the world sharing her experience with churches, nonprofits, and universities. She procrastinates in Northern California, where she lives with her family, two dumb dogs, and an evil cat.

Website: theveryworstmissionary.com
Facebook: jamietheverywdorstmissionary
Twitter/Instagram: @jamiethevwm
Booking: chaffeemanagment.com/jamie-wright